Barrier-Free Travel

the

GRAND CANYON

for Wheelers and Slow Walkers

Candy B. Harrington

PHOTOGRAPHS BY

CHARLES PANNELL

CANDY & CHARLES CREATIVE CONCEPTS

ISBN: 978-0-9985103-5-4

Candy & Charles Creative Concepts
PO Box 278
Ripon, CA 95366-0278

To Charles

Contents

Preface

The Grand Canyon and Beyond

We were most definitely lost.

There I was in the middle of the desert staring at a locked gate and re-reading my printed directions. Charles was tapping the steering wheel impatiently, awaiting further navigational instructions and looking anxiously in my direction. "Let me call," I stammered; but when I peered at my phone I saw the dreaded "no service" screen.

Then out of the corner of my eye I spied a lady standing on her porch in the distance waving at us. I just figured it was a friendly community, so I waved back. Then she motioned for us to come up the hill toward her house, so off we went. Charles rolled down his window and the neighbor lady smiled and queried, "Are you looking for the Airbnb? We nodded in unison like a pair of baby chicks.

Then she jumped in with her animated directions, complete with hand signals. We both kind of just stared blankly at her, with a mutual look of bewilderment on our faces. Our welcome wagon savior stopped mid-sentence, stared quizzically at us and very slowly asked, "Do you speak English, honey?" I looked down at my directions and sputtered, "Um yes, but, but, but our directions say to go another way, and...". She cut me off mid-sputter. "Well that's all well and good, but that's not how things work in this town," she emphatically replied. And she proceeded with her animated directions.

In the end we found our cottage and had a good laugh that night. And that's what a road trip is all about — an adventure to remember. It wasn't the first time we took a wrong turn — on that or any road trip — and it most certainly wouldn't be the last either.

So when I sat down to outline the second edition of this book, I thought back on some of our more memorable road trip wrong turns and adventures, and I realized that I needed to expand the scope of this title. After all, the main way people get to the Grand Canyon is by vehicle; and with remnants of Route 66 and a bevy of kitschy attractions along Interstate 40 from Kingman to Winslow, it just makes sense to also include them in the second edition. And of course, if you're going to make a real road trip out of it, you also need information about accessible dining and lodging options along the way, so those listings made the cut as well.

But that isn't the only reason for a second edition of this popular access guide.

It's been five years since the publication of the first edition of this book, and in that time I've seen more than a few changes in what's often been described as "America's favorite national park."

For starters, there's the expansion of the accessible multiuse Greenway Trail on the South Rim. Although this project took years to complete, it was definitely worth the wait.

Additionally, on my previous visit a good portion of the Rim Trail from the South Kaibab Trailhead to Hermit Road was accessible; however there were still some steps, bumps and steep sections along the way. I'm happy to report that those access obstacles have been removed, and there's now a contiguous five-mile accessible trail along the South Rim. Again, this was a multi-year project, but I'm excited to share this improvement with my readers.

Accessible shuttle service continues to be the norm in the park — and it's even been expanded to Tusayan. So now you can stay in an accessible hotel in Tusayan — I've covered those in this edition too — and leave the driving to someone else.

Additionally, I'm thrilled to report that more South Rim improvements are also on the drawing board. As aging properties are renovated, access obstacles — like steps — are removed. Historic Bright Angel Lodge now has an accessible front entrance, complete with automatic doors. And Maswik South will be razed and replaced with a new — and undoubtedly more accessible — incarnation.

Access has also improved on the North Rim, where some of the "semi-accessible" cabins that I looked at five years ago have been converted to fully accessible units. Now that's a step in the right direction for sure.

Grand Canyon West has also seen a few improvements since my last visit, including the completion of the Diamond Bar Road paving project. They've also added a new restaurant, and their entire fleet of shuttle buses is now lift-equipped.

So between these changes and the new section of the book, an update was definitely in order. And there's just no better time to release this expanded edition than on the 100th birthday of Grand Canyon National Park — February 26, 2019.

So get ready to explore all that the Grand Canyon has to offer. Plan a road trip and drive along a few remaining stretches of the Mother Road, ride a historic train, explore red rock country or just go and stand on the corner in Winslow, Arizona. Getting there is truly half the fun, and this book will help you do that in a very accessible way.

And if you spot some changes along your journey, be sure and let me know so I can post them on www.BarrierFreeGrandCanyon.com.

Enjoy this beautiful national park — and let me know how your trip went!

Candy Harrington
candy@EmergingHorizons.com
www.CandyHarrington.com
www.EmergingHorizons.com
Facebook: Candy Harrington
Twitter: Candy B. Harrington
Pinterest: Candy Harrington

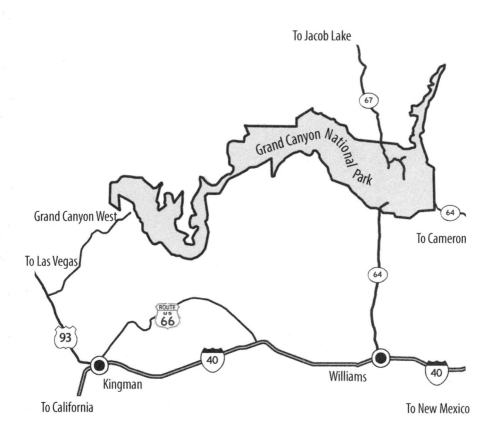

To Jacob Lake

67

Grand Canyon National Park

64

To Cameron

Grand Canyon West

To Las Vegas

64

ROUTE
US
66

93

40

Williams

40

Kingman

To California

To New Mexico

Admission, Reservations and Park Passes

Admission Fees

The admission fee to Grand Canyon National Park is $35 per car. This fee is collected at park entrance stations, and admission is good for seven days. Payment can be made with cash or a credit card. Save your receipt as you'll need to show it if you enter a park through a different gate, or if you come and go from a park.

Visitors traveling to the South Rim can also purchase an entrance permit at the following locations.

Flagstaff Visitor Center
Williams Visitor Center
Valle Chevron Travel Stop

National Geographic Visitor Center, Tusayan
Grand Canyon Chamber of Commerce, Tusayan
R.P.'s Stage Stop, Tusayan
Red Feather Lodge, Tusayan
Canyon Plaza Resort, Tusayan

Plan ahead, and get your entrance permit in advance, to save time at the entrance station.

The National Park Service also offers free admission on several days throughout the year, including Martin Luther King, Jr. Day, National Public Lands Day, Veterans Day and the first day of National Park Week. It's best to arrive early on these days, as the park is usually quite crowded.

Park Passes

A number of discount park passes are also available at all national park entrance kiosks. See if you qualify for one, as it may help trim your travel budget.

Access Pass

This free lifetime pass provides for free admission to all national parks, and is available to U.S. citizens or residents with a permanent disability. Applicants must provide documentation of a permanent disability, and prove residency or citizenship. The pass also offers a 50% discount on campsites and boat launch fees. It generally does not provide for a discount on fees charged by concessionaires.

Military Pass

The free annual Military Pass provides for free park admission, and is available to active members of the Army, Navy, Air Force, Marines and Coast Guard. Reserve and National Guard Members are also eligible. A Common Access Card or Military ID (Form 1173) is required to obtain this pass.

Senior Pass

This lifetime pass provides free park admission, and is available to U.S. citizens or permanent residents age 62 or older. The cost of the pass is $80. An annual Senior Pass is also available for $20, and the cost for this annual pass can be applied to the purchase of a lifetime pass. Proof of age and residency or citizenship are required. The pass also offers a 50% discount on campsites and boat launch fees. It generally does not provide for a discount on fees charged by concessionaires.

Annual Pass

If you plan on visiting a number of national parks throughout the year, the Annual Pass may be a good deal for you. This non-transferable pass costs $80 and it's good for free park admission to all national parks for the entire year. It's an especially attractive deal if you live near a national park, or are planning a road trip that includes a number of national parks. You can also order this pass by calling (888) 275-8747.

Annual 4th Grade Pass

This free annual pass is available to all 4th graders and is valid for the duration of the 4th grade school year and the following summer. Paper vouchers can be obtained at www.everykidinapark.gov and exchanged for an Annual 4th Grade Pass at any national park entrance. This pass is also available to home-schooled students.

Grand Canyon National Park Annual Pass

If you're planning several trips to the Grand Canyon within a year, the Grand Canyon National Park Annual Pass could save you a few bucks. It costs $70 and it's valid for 12 months from the date of purchase. It's good for unlimited visits to Grand Canyon National Park for the purchaser and others in the vehicle.

Information

Although there is a variety of contact information listed for each national park in the resources sections at the end of the chapters, the social media contacts are particularly important. In my experience — and that of my readers — the parks are quite responsive to inquiries received via social media; so if you have a time sensitive question I recommend either posting it on their Twitter or Facebook feed, or using Facebook to send a private message to them.

Authorized Park Concessionaires

All of the lodgings inside Grand Canyon National Park are operated by authorized concessionaires, who have contracted with the National Park Service, and operate under strict guidelines. They are responsible for the daily operations of the facilities, as well as improvements and upgrades. It's important to deal with these concessionaires directly when you make a reservation; as not only will you get the best price there, but you will also have access to employees that can block the accessible rooms and describe the access details of each available room. Unfortunately these concessionaires do not always come up first in internet searches because paid advertisements appear before them. Some of these paid advertisements even list "national park lodges" that are located many miles outside the parks, which is very misleading to people who are unfamiliar with the geography of the parks. The authorized concessionaires in Grand Canyon National Park are listed below. Again, deal directly with these concessionaires for all lodging reservations.

Grand Canyon National Park Concessionaires

Xanterra

(888) 297-2757

www.grandcanyonlodges.com

www.facebook.com/grandcanyonlodges

    El Tovar Hotel

    Thunderbird Lodge

    Kachina Lodge

    Maswick Lodge

Delaware North

(877) 404-4611

www.visitgrandcanyon.com

www.facebook.com/visitgrandcanyon

    Yavapai Lodge

Forever Resorts

(877) 386-4383

www.grandcanyonforever.com

www.facebook.com/GrandCanyonNorthRim

    Grand Canyon Lodge North Rim

Grand Canyon National Park

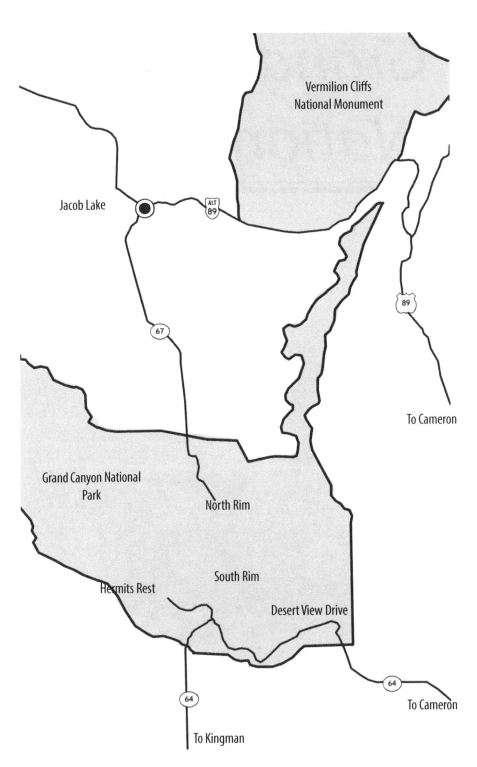

Vermilion Cliffs
National Monument

Jacob Lake

ALT
89

67

89

To Cameron

Grand Canyon National
Park

North Rim

South Rim

Hermits Rest

Desert View Drive

64

To Cameron

64

To Kingman

Covering about 1,900 square miles in Northern Arizona, the Grand Canyon became a national park on Feb 26, 1919. The canyon itself is 277 miles long, a mile deep and up to 18 miles across at its widest point. And although it took approximately 3 to 6 million years to form, the forces of nature continue to work to alter the canyon's contour today.

There are three entrances to Grand Canyon National Park.

The busy South Entrance is located on Highway 64 near Tusayan, about an hour-drive from Williams.

The East Entrance is located on the east side of Desert View Drive, 25 miles east of Grand Canyon Village, and 30 miles west of Cameron on Highway 64.

The North Entrance is located 30 miles south of Jacob Lake on Highway 67.

Even though much of the park is rugged back country, there's still a wide variety of accessible trails, attractions, scenic drives and lodging options in the park. So today — 100 years after this spectacular canyon was set aside as a national treasure — Grand Canyon National Park truly is accessible to everyone.

View from Grand Canyon Lodge North Rim

The Basics

Road Conditions and Operating Seasons

The South Rim is open year round; however Desert View Drive and Hermit Road are usually closed after snowstorms, until the snow plows have cleared the roads. There are no vehicle restrictions on South Rim roads, but parking is limited for RVs and trailers, especially those over 22 feet long. Additionally, the parking lots for passenger vehicles usually fill up by mid-morning, especially on weekends and holidays in the summer. The best plan of action is to arrive early, or park in Tusayan and take the free park shuttle to the Grand Canyon Visitor Center on the South Rim.

The North Rim is only open part of the year, and the road is not plowed in the winter. Most of the facilities in the park close on October 15 and reopen on May 15. Between October 15 and October 31, the north Rim Campground is open but it has limited services. Between November 1 and December 1, the road remains open from dusk to dawn; however if snow closes Highway 67 the park will also close. For more information on current road conditions, call (928) 638-7496.

During the summer months, the weather is warm, but the high elevation and low humidity can cause dramatic temperature shifts from day to night. Lightening is also common during the summer monsoon season. The spring and fall weather is extremely volatile, and snow is even possible in May and October. Winter snowstorms are common on the canyon rims, and it's a good idea to travel with chains or cables.

Weather updates are available on the park's Facebook page and Twitter feed.

Altitude

Elevations along the canyon rim range from 7,000 feet to 8,000 feet. The highest viewpoint on the South Rim is Navajo Point (7,498 feet); but the top of Desert Watchtower — which is only accessible by stairs — is technically the highest point on the South Rim, with an elevation of 7,522 feet. The highest point on the North Rim is Point Imperial, which has an elevation of 8,803 feet.

Although the symptoms of altitude sickness generally do not appear at elevations under 8,000 feet, wheelchair-users, slow walkers and people with compromised immune systems may feel the effects of increased altitudes at significantly lower elevations. Symptoms can include headaches, dizziness, shortness of breath, lethargy, insomnia and gastrointestinal disturbances. If you are unfamiliar with the effects that higher elevations have on your body, it's best to take it slow and drink plenty of water for the first few days at any increased elevation, especially if you live at sea level. Additionally, you may want to consult your doctor regarding the effects that increased elevations may have on your specific condition. To assist you in your travel planning, elevations are noted at the beginning of each section.

Airports

Although Grand Canyon National Park Airport (GCN) is located just seven miles from the South Rim in Tusayan, air operations there are limited to helicopter flights and fixed-wing aircraft tours of the canyon. The closest airport to Grand Canyon National Park with commercial service is Flagstaff Pulliam Airport (FLG), which is a 90-minute drive from the South Entrance. It offers daily flights to Phoenix on American Airlines. Accessible van rentals are available in Flagstaff and at Phoenix Sky Harbor International Airport from Access Mobility of Arizona (www. wheelersvanrentals.com, 888-859-8880). Advance reservations are required for accessible van rentals.

Amtrak

The Amtrak Southwest Chief, which offers daily service between Chicago and Los Angeles, stops in Flagstaff and Williams. The stations are both wheelchair-accessible with no barriers between the stations and the trains. Free accessible transfers are provided to Grand Canyon Railway passengers from the Williams Amtrak Station to the Grand Canyon Railway Station (and hotel) in Williams. Reservations are required and are available through Grand Canyon Railway. Accessible shuttle service from Flagstaff to the South Rim is available through Arizona Shuttle.

Arizona Shuttle

(928)350-8466
www.arizonashuttle.com

Arizona Shuttle provides accessible transfers between the Flagstaff Amtrak Station and Maswik Lodge on the South Rim, The shuttle stops at Flagstaff Pulliam Airport, the Grand Canyon Railway Hotel in Williams, and the Imax Theater in Tusayan. Accessible vehicle requests must be made by phone, at least 24 hours in advance.

Park Shuttle

Although personal vehicles are permitted on many of the South Rim roads, free shuttle bus transportation is also available. During peak visitation times the park gets quite crowded, and with limited parking at some of the popular sights and trailheads, it just makes sense to park your car and take the shuttle bus. All shuttle buses are equipped with ramps and they can kneel to accommodate slow walkers; however they cannot accommodate wheelchairs larger than 30 inches wide or 48 inches long. They also can't accommodate most scooters.

There are three shuttle bus routes along the South Rim — the Village Route, the Hermits Rest Route and the Kaibab Rim Route. The Village Route shuttle stops at the Grand Canyon Visitor Center, the campground and the South Rim hotels, and it takes 50 minutes to complete the entire loop. The Kaibab Rim Route shuttle stops at the Grand Canyon Visitor Center, Mather Point, the Yavapai Geology Museum, Yaki Point, Pipe Creek Vista and the South Kaibab Trailhead. It also takes 50 minutes to complete the entire loop. The Hermits Rest shuttle stops at the overlooks and trailheads along Hermit Road on an 80-minute loop. This route only operates from March 1 to November 30.

There's also a shuttle that runs from the Tusayan Imax Theater to the Grand Canyon Visitor Center on the South Rim. This route operates from March 1 to September 30. Visitors can park their cars anywhere in Tusayan, hop on the shuttle and skip the lines at the South Entrance during this busy season. The Tusayan Route operates on a 40 minute round-trip schedule, and it stops at the Best Western Grand Squire Inn, The Grand Hotel, and the Big E Steakhouse & Saloon. There is no fee to ride this shuttle, but visitors must show a park pass or an entrance receipt in order to board the bus.

A shuttle bus map is included in the pocket map, which is available at the visitors centers and the park entrance stations.

Xanterra Taxi

Xanterra Resorts operates a taxi service which serves Grand Canyon Village and Tusayan. Accessible taxis are available upon request 24 hours a day. Advance reservations are not available, but it's usually only a short wait for a vehicle. Taxis can be ordered by phone at (928) 638-2822 or (928) 638-2631 ext. 6563, or in person at the front desk at any Xanterra South Rim property.

Scenic Drive Accessibility Permit

A special Scenic Drive Accessibility Permit is available to anybody who has mobility issues, and may have problems boarding the park shuttle buses. The permit, which must be prominently displayed, grants users access to Hermit Road and Yaki Point Road, which have restrictions on private vehicle usage. Hermit Road is closed to private vehicles from March 1 to November 30; and Yaki Point Road and the Kaibab Trailhead parking lot are closed to private vehicles all year. There is no fee for the permit, which is available at park entrances, visitor centers and park hotels. A disabled placard is not required in order to obtain this permit; however vehicles are prohibited from parking in accessible parking places in the park without a disabled placard or license plate. The Scenic Drive Accessibility Permit is only valid for driving on the restricted roads.

Xanterra Bus Tours

(888) 297-2757
www.grandcanyonlodges.com

Xanterra offers a number of narrated bus tours that depart from Grand Canyon Village on the South Rim. Accessible buses are available with 48-hours advance notice, but it's best to reserve space as far in advance as possible, as these popular tours fill up quickly.

Sunrise Tour

The one-and-a-half-hour Sunrise Tour covers the west end of the park, and focuses on the geology of the canyon. While waiting for the sunrise at Hopi Point or a nearby overlook, the guide answers questions, and even point outs the best vantage points for sunrise photos. It's the perfect way to start a Grand Canyon day.

Hermits Rest Tour

The two-hour Hermits Rest Tour travels along this old wagon road built by the Santa Fe Railway. The tour stops at Hermits Rest, as well as several other viewpoints along the way.

Desert View Tour

The Desert View Tour takes nearly four hours, as it covers the entire length of Desert View Drive. The tour stops at Lipan Point, for a spectacular view of the Colorado River, as well as Desert View, the location of the historic Watchtower. It's a good way to see this area or the park if you don't have a car.

Sunset Tour

The one-and-a-half-hour Sunset Tour offers a good introduction to the South Rim, as it includes an overview of the village area and the historic architecture of Mary Elizabeth Jane Colter. It also touches on the human history of the Grand Canyon. The highlight of the tour is the sunset at Yaki Point or Mohave Point, two of the most panoramic South Rim viewpoints.

Connectivity

Some carriers offer cell phone service on the South Rim, however signal strength varies by location. Additionally, even though coverage may be available, the circuits could be overloaded due to the traffic volume. Wi-Fi is available to guests in the hotel lobbies, and to everyone at Canyon Village Market & Deli (signal strength varies), the library and at Park Headquarters. On the North Rim, coverage is spotty as well, and it's carrier-dependent; and like on the South Rim the circuits are often overloaded. The only free public Wi-Fi is available at the General Store. Best bet is to just unplug and enjoy the scenery.

Wheelchairs

Wheelchairs are available for rent at Bright Angel Bicycles, which is located next to the Grand Canyon Visitor Center on the South Rim. Tandem bicycles are also available there. For more information call (928) 814-8704 or visit www.bikegrandcanyon.com.

Wheelchairs are available for loan on a first-come basis at the North Rim Visitor Center.

Ranger Programs

Free ranger programs and hikes are presented at the Yavapai Geology Museum, the Tusayan Museum, the Shrine of the Ages, and the North Rim Visitor Center; while evening programs are held at McKee Amphitheater, Mather Campground, Grand Canyon Lodge North Rim and the North Rim Campground. A schedule of all programs is available at the visitor center. Access details to all of the program venues are contained in this book.

Camping

Reservations for accessible campsites at Mather Campground and the North Rim Campground can be made up to six months in advance at www.recreation.gov or (877) 444-6777. Reservations for accessible sites may require proof of disability upon arrival. If nobody has a need for an accessible site, able-bodied campers may be asked to move to a non-accessible site if a qualified person with a disability has a need for the accessible site. Accessible sites may not be reserved by able-bodied campers unless they are the only sites left at the time of reservation.

Campsites at the Desert View Campground are only available on a walk-in basis.

Trailer Village is the only campground in the park that offers full RV hookups. It's operated by Delaware North, and campsites can be reserved at www.visitgrandcanyon.com or (877) 404-4611.

Service Animals

There are some restrictions on pets in Grand Canyon National Park; however service animals — as defined in the Americans with Disabilities Act (ADA) — are permitted in all areas of the park, including public buildings, lodges and shuttle buses. Under the ADA, a service animal is defined as a dog that is individually trained to do work or preform a task for a disabled person. Furthermore the work or task that the dog provides must be directly related to the person's disability. Dogs whose sole function is to provide comfort or emotional support — Emotional Support Animals — do not qualify as service animals under the ADA or in Grand Canyon National Park. Emotional Support Animals are subject to the park's pet regulations and restrictions.

It should also be noted that although some organizations sell "service animal registration" documents on-line, these documents do not convey any rights under the ADA, and the Department of Justice does not recognize them as proof that a dog is a service animal.

For more information on the ADA definition of a service animal, visit www.ada.gov.

While in Grand Canyon National Park, service animals must be leashed at all times, must not disturb wildlife and must not be excessively noisy. It is the owner's responsibility to clean up and properly dispose of all excrement left by their service animal.

Service animals in training are not recognized as service animals in Grand Canyon National Park, and are therefore subject to the park's pet regulations and restrictions.

On the South Rim, pets are prohibited on trails below the rim, on park shuttle buses, and in the lodges (except for Yavapai Lodge which has some pet friendly rooms). Pets must always be kept on a maximum six-foot long leash, and never left unattended.

On the North Rim, leashed pets are only allowed on the greenway that connects the North Kaibab Trail to the park entrance station.

Xanterra operates a kennel on the South Rim, near Maswik Lodge. For more information call (928) 638-0534, or visit www.grandcanyonlodges.com. There is no kennel on the North Rim.

South Rim

L ocated just 60 miles north of Williams on Highway 64, the South Rim of the Grand Canyon includes Grand Canyon Village, one of the most touristed sections of the park. On the plus side, this area also offers a large selection of accessible lodging options, several accessible trails, and a nice variety of visitor services. And since an accessible shuttle bus stops at all the major sights it's an excellent option for visitors who don't have a vehicle. There are accessible vault toilets located near the South Entrance kiosk, on the right near the Grand Canyon National Park sign. The south entrance is located six miles from Tusayan.

Attractions

Grand Canyon Visitor Center

The closest accessible parking to the Grand Canyon Visitor Center is located in Parking Area 2. There's a level pathway from the parking lot over to the shuttle bus stop and the visitor center. Accessible restrooms are located near the shuttle bus stop and next to the visitor center. There is barrier-free access inside the visitor center, which offers interpretive exhibits and a ranger information desk. There's level
Grand Canyon Visitor Center

17

access to the 20-minute movie, *Grand Canyon: A Journey of Wonder*, which is shown on the hour and half-hour. Accessible seating and companion seats are available in the theater. There's also level access to the Grand Canyon Association Park Store, which is located across from the visitor center.

Mather Point

Mather Point is one of the best places for sunrise views of the canyon; but to be honest, the views of the Colorado River and the South Kaibab Trail below are great throughout the day. There's a paved path from the visitor center out to one Mather Point overlook, but that route does have a slight incline, and it's not a good choice for slow walkers who can't manage any distance. That said, the accessible parking spaces in Parking Area 1 are only 100 feet from another Mather Point overlook. — and that route is fairly level. From the first overlook, it's just a short level walk past the amphitheater to the second overlook.

Yavapai Geology Museum

Perched on the canyon rim, the Yavapai Geology Museum features level access with plenty of room to maneuver a wheelchair inside. The building was constructed in the 1920s, when a group of geologists chose this site as the best representation of Grand Canyon geology. Today the structure houses exhibits about the geology of the area, and offers a great canyon

Mather Point on the South Rim

view. Accessible restrooms are located near the parking lot (just follow the sign), and there are also benches to sit down and rest inside the museum.

Verkamp's Visitor Center

This 1906 building was once the home to John Verkamp's curio shop, where he hawked souvenirs to Grand Canyon visitors. Today it houses an information desk and a book store, along with some interpretive exhibits that trace the history of the park, from 1870 to the present day. The building features ramp access, with plenty of room to navigate a wheelchair inside. Accessible restrooms are located behind the building.

Hopi House

Built in 1905, Hopi House was the first of eight Mary Colter-designed buildings in the park. The large multi-story building resembles a Hopi pueblo, and it houses a gift shop filled with Native American wares, including a large selection of jewelry, pottery and baskets. The north (canyon side) entrance is accessible, and there is barrier-free access to most of the first-floor areas. One section of the first floor has a few steps down, with no ramp access; and the second floor can only be accessed by a stairway.

Bright Angel History Room

The Bright Angel History Room is located just off the lobby of the Bright Angel Hotel. There is level access to the room through a wide doorway, and

Hopi House

plenty of space to maneuver a wheelchair around the exhibits that illustrate the history of the Fred Harvey Company, El Tovar Hotel and Bright Angel Lodge. Exhibits include artifacts from these two Harvey Houses, as well as old photos, an 1880 Harvey House dinner gong, and even a vintage Harvey Girl uniform. It also includes information and photos about the Harvey Indian Detour excursion, which took train passengers on a five-night trip to nearby Native American sites. Both the canyon entrance and the main entrance of the Bright Angel Hotel are wheelchair-accessible.

Lookout Studio

Lookout Studio was designed in 1914 by Mary Colter, as a gift shop and lookout point for guests of the Fred Harvey Company. There is level access and a wide doorway to the first floor of this rubblestone building, which is precariously perched on the canyon rim. Inside you'll find a small gift shop, and limited views of the canyon. The best views of the canyon are from the front terrace, which can only be accessed by a stairway.

Mather Point Amphitheater

There's level access to this amphitheater from the accessible parking spaces in Parking Area 1. As an added bonus, the amphitheater also overlooks the canyon and offers spectacular views. Accessible seating is located in front, with companion seats nearby.

Lookout Studio

Shrine of the Ages

This multipurpose building, which is located next to Park Headquarters is used for meetings, special events, ranger programs and non-denominational church services. Accessible parking is located in front of the building. There's level access to the entrance, and barrier-free access inside. Both eastbound and westbound shuttle buses stop there.

McKee Amphitheater

The McKee Amphitheater is located behind the Park Headquarters building, however the paved trail from Parking Lot A is too steep for most wheelers and slow walkers. The most accessible way to get to this amphitheater is to park in the employee lot on the other side of Park Headquarters. There's no accessible parking in this level lot, and there are a few bumps (in place of a curb-cut) up to the path; however the path itself is level. If you can get there, the amphitheater has plenty of room for wheelchairs in the back, front and on the sides.

Village Amphitheater

There's level access to this small amphitheater, which is located between Kachina Lodge and Thunderbird Lodge. Accessible seating is available in the front row.

Trails

Greenway Trail (Eastern Section)

This nicely accessible paved trail features some undulations, but it has a maximum grade of 1:8 with a number of level spots along the way. The slight elevation changes make this multiuse trail interesting; however it's not entirely level like the central section of the Rim Trail. Still it's an excellent choice for many wheelers and slow walkers, as well as a good option for handcyclists.

The trail begins across the parking lot from the South Kaibab Trailhead. From there it's a 1-mile walk through the forest to Pipe Creek Vista, and another mile to an intersection where the trail forks off to the left and heads over to the Grand Canyon Visitor Center. After that it continues through the forest along the road to Market Plaza and Village East, before it winds past the mule barn and ends at the beginning of Hermit Road.

Another branch of this section of the Greenway Trail runs from the Grand Canyon Visitor Center to Trailer Village (.7 mile), and Mather Campground (1.2 miles), before it exits the park and continues on another 6.6 miles to Tusayan.

Rim Trail

The Rim Trail travels along the canyon edge from the South Kaibab Trailhead on the east to Hermit Road on the West. Although there are some undulations along the eastern section of the trail, the entire five miles is now wheelchair-accessible. Bicycles and handcycles are not permitted along the Rim Trail, except for the far eastern section, which is also part of the Greenway Trail. Additionally, there are shuttle bus stops near Pipe Creek Vista, Mather Point and the Yavapai Geology Museum so it's easy to do shorter portions of this trail.

The Rim Trail begins across the street from the shuttle bus stop at South Kaibab Trailhead and travels west for a mile to Pipe Creek Vista. From there it's another mile to an intersection where the trail branches off to the right and skirts the rim for a half-mile out to Mather Point. After that the Rim Trail continues along for .7-mile to the Yavapai Geology Museum, where parts of it then transition to the accessible Trail of Time.

The 1.3-mile Trail of Time follows the canyon rim from the Yavapai Geology Museum to Verkamp's Visitor Center. This paved level trail helps visitors understand the magnitude of geologic time. The geologic timeline is marked by brass medallions embedded in the pavement; while interpretive exhibits and displays along the way encourage visitors to connect the visible rocks in the canyon to the geologic timeline. Wheelchair-height viewing scopes are available and accessible pictograms point out the wheelchair-accessible route.

View along the Greenway Trail

It should be noted that it's essential to follow these pictograms, as parts of the original inaccessible Rim Trail still branch off out to the canyon edge.

The Trail of Time transitions back to the accessible Rim Trail at Verkamp's Visitor Center, where it travels a half-mile along the canyon rim in front of Hopi House, the El Tovar Hotel, Kachina Lodge, Thunderbird Lodge, the Arizona Room and Bright Angel Lodge. This central section of the trail is wide, paved and level; and it's probably the most crowded trail in the park. That said, it's a great place to get a canyon view if you can't walk very far, as it's just a few steps from many of the South Rim hotels. After that the trail continues past Kolb Studio for another .6-mile before it passes the Bright Angel Trailhead (which boasts accessible restrooms), and ends at the shuttle bus stop at the beginning of Hermit Road.

Greenway Trail (Hermit Road)
The Hermit Road section of the Greenway Trail runs from Monument Creek Vista to Hermits Rest, along the canyon on Hermit Road. This 2.8-mile trail is paved, with an average grade of 4%. The 1.7-mile section from Monument Creek Vista to Pima Point winds through a pinion and juniper woodland and features accessible overlooks along the way. The 1.1-mile stretch from Pima Point to Hermits Rest connects to the paved Rim Trail (where bicycles are prohibited) at the .7 mile point. From there, cyclists are directed to the bicycle lane that runs along Hermit Road.

Spotting scope on the Trail of Time

Scenic Drives

Hermit Road

Hermit Road, which is located on the west end of the South Rim, follows the canyon rim and ends at Hermits Rest. This seven-mile drive can be done in a private vehicle or on a park shuttle bus, depending on the time of year.

The route is closed to private vehicles from March 1 to November 30, but visitors who are unable to access the park shuttle buses can get a Scenic Drive Accessibility Permit and drive their own vehicles along the route during that time.

There are nine canyon overlooks along Hermit Road; and although the shuttle bus stops at all the overlooks on the westbound route, it only stops at Pima Point, Mohave Point and Powell Point on the eastbound route. Remember to pack along plenty of water too, as water bottles can only be refilled at Hermits Rest. And if you're up for a little hike, get off at Monument Creek Vista and take the accessible Hermit Road Greenway Trail to Pima Point or Hermits Rest. It's also a good idea to get an early start on this drive for a more relaxed view of the canyon, as this popular route gets crowded in the afternoons.

Trailview Overlook

Located just .7 mile from the Village Route Transfer shuttle bus stop,
View along the Hermit Road section of the Greenway Trail

Trailview Overlook features good views of Grand Canyon Village and the Bright Angel Trail. There are steps down to the lower overlook, but the view is still good from the upper area. If you look real hard, you may be able to spot hikers and mules moving along the Bright Angel Trail below.

Maricopa Point

A wide level asphalt trails leads 150 yards, from the shuttle bus stop out to the overlook, where you can view the Orphan Mine site. This mine first operated as a copper mine from 1891 to 1936; then when a high-grade uranium deposit was discovered in 1951, a private mining company purchased the claim. The uranium mine ceased operation in 1969, and the claim reverted back to the federal government in 1987.

Powell Point

There is a paved level trail out to the overlook at Powell Point, with benches to sit and enjoy the canyon view at the end. There is also a monument dedicated to Major John Wesley Powell, who led the first documented expedition through the Grand Canyon in 1869. The monument has steps up to the top; however the view is just as good from the overlook in front of the monument.

Maricopa Point

Hopi Point

Hopi Point is the highest point along Hermit Road. It's also a very popular stop for motorcoaches, so it can get pretty crowded. Accessible restrooms are located in the parking lot, and there is ramp access out to the overlook from the left side of the parking lot. The overlook offers a good view of the Colorado River, but the noise from the motorcoaches and the passengers tends to detract from it a bit.

Mohave Point

Mohave Point features some good canyon views as well as a glimpse of the Colorado River. An accessible quarter-mile paved pathway leads around to several canyon viewpoints before it loops back to the shuttle bus stop. This stop is also a good place to enjoy a Grand Canyon sunrise or sunset.

The Abyss

The Abyss is aptly name, as it features a 3,000-foot sheer drop-off into the canyon. There is a good view of the canyon and the Colorado River, from the shuttle bus stop all the way out to the viewpoint; however, you have to walk over some rough rock and gravel to get all the way out to the end of the overlook.

Monument Creek Vista

Although there is a step down to the overlook, you can get a good view of Monument Creek from the shuttle bus stop. This is also the starting point for the 1.7-mile accessible Greenway Trail to Pima Point.

Hopi Point

Pima Point

There is level access from the shuttle bus stop to the overlook, which features a good view of Monument Creek Canyon and a piece of the Colorado River. The path that is furthest from the bus stop also leads out to the overlook, however it has a step down. From Pima Point, the accessible Greenway Trail continues for another 1.1 miles to Hermits Rest.

Hermits Rest

Hermits Rest, which was designed by Mary Colter as a rest stop for canyon tourists, is the last stop along Hermit Road. There is level access from the shuttle bus stop down to Hermits Rest, however there are steps leading up into this 1914 building. Inside there is a gift shop and a snack bar, however this National Register of Historic Places building is not wheelchair-accessible. Accessible restrooms are located near the shuttle bus stop. There is also level access to the iconic Hermits Rest Arch, which is located half-way between the restrooms and the shuttle bus stop.

Kaibab Rim

Kaibab Rim, which is located on the east side of the South Rim, also offers several scenic canyon views and overlooks. Private vehicles are prohibited along Yaki Point Road, which offers access to the rim; but visitors who are unable to access the park shuttle buses can get a Scenic Drive Accessibility Permit, and drive their own vehicles along the road.

View from the Kaibab Rim

The Kaibab Rim shuttle bus departs from the Grand Canyon Visitor Center, Mather Point and the Yavapai Geology Museum and stops at all three overlooks along this scenic drive.

Yaki Point

Yaki Point offers some nice windshield views of the canyon, and it's a popular alternative to Mather Point for sunrise views. Best bet is to get an accessible driving permit and drive down for sunrise, to avoid the crowds on the early morning shuttle bus.

South Kaibab Trailhead

The Rim Trail and Greenway Trail start across the street from the shuttle bus stop. Even if you can't manage the entire mile jaunt to Pipe Creek Vista, go around the corner of the trail to the first overlook for a great canyon view. Accessible vault toilets are located near the shuttle bus stop.

Pipe Creek Vista

There's a level pathway along Pipe Creek Vista, which offers a panoramic view of the canyon. You can also continue along the Rim Trail to Mather Point, or just do a short out-and-back stroll and take the shuttle bus back to Grand Canyon Village.

The Greenway Trail to Pipe Creek Vista

Lodging

There are six properties on the South Rim, five of which have accessible rooms. El Tovar Hotel, Kachina Lodge and Thunderbird Lodge are located directly on the rim, while Maswik Lodge is about a quarter-mile away. Yavapai Lodge is located near Market Plaza, which is just a short shuttle bus ride from the rim. All of the South Rim properties are open year-round. And although access details for each property are included in the following section, here are a few handy lodging tips to help you find a room that meets your needs.

Accessible parking is available at all South Rim properties, but it may be difficult to find. The best plan of action is to park in the loading zone in front of the property for registration. From there, front desk personnel will provide a map, with directions to the closest accessible parking areas.

Peak season runs from President's Day to the beginning of November, so plan ahead.

Portable shower chairs are also available for standard rooms, so make sure and request one when you make your reservation.

Medicine refrigerators are available upon advance request, for rooms that lack standard refrigerators.

All accessible rooms are located on the first floor, so requests for upper floor accessible room cannot be honored.

Kachina Lodge is the only property with an elevator, so it's a good choice for slow walkers who want an upper floor standard room, but cannot do stairs.

El Tovar Hotel has a limited number of ground floor standard rooms that may work for some slow walkers, however they all have a step up into the bathroom.

Kachina Lodge and Thunderbird Lodge have steps along the first-floor corridors, so slow walkers who want a standard ground floor room need to ask for a room along an accessible route.

There are no accessible rooms at Bright Angel Lodge or Yavapai West; however all of the rooms at Yavapai West are on one level.

All of the South Rim properties are air conditioned, except Yavapai West, Maswik South and Bright Angel Lodge.

Accessible rooms should be reserved three-to-four months in advance; however if you want an accessible room with a canyon view you should reserve it as soon as the reservation period opens up, which is 13 months in advance.

Last but not least, make sure and disclose all of your access needs to the reservation agent, so you can get an accessible room with the specific features that you need.

El Tovar Hotel

1 El Tovar Road
Grand Canyon, AZ 86023
(888) 297-2757
www.grandcanyonlodges.com

The El Tovar Hotel dates back to 1905, making it the oldest property in the park. It's considered the premier lodging facility at the Grand Canyon, and it has hosted Theodore Roosevelt, Albert Einstein and Zane Grey. This National Historic Landmark has been renovated many times over the years, and today it has wheelchair-accessible rooms with tub/shower combinations.

The main entrance (which faces Hopi House) has steps, but a ramped accessible entrance is located on the canyon side. Just head towards the flagpole, and turn left when you get to the end of the building.

There's good pathway access to the front desk, and level access to the accessible rooms, which are located down a hallway off the main lobby. The *Bedroom in room 6439 at the El Tovar Lodge*

Bathroom in room 6439 at the El Tovar Lodge

El Tovar Hotel has two wheelchair-accessible rooms.

Room 6439 has wide doorways, a lowered peephole, low-pile carpet and good pathway access. It's furnished with a 27-inch high king-sized bed with wheelchair access on both sides, two night stands and a refrigerator. There's an accessible pathway to the bathroom, which is equipped with a tub/shower combination, with grab bars, a hand-held showerhead and a portable shower chair. The bathroom also includes a toilet with grab bars on the back and left walls (as seated), and a pedestal sink.

Room 6441 includes the same basic access features as room 6439, but it's a deluxe room and it's a little larger. It's furnished with two 28-inch high queen-sized beds with wheelchair access between them. The bathroom configuration is the same as in room 6439, except that the toilet grab bars are located on the back and right walls (as seated).

There's good pathway access to the public areas of the property as well, including the lobby, dining room and bar. Accessible restrooms are located in the lobby, and a key is available at the front desk.

Bedroom in room 6441 at the El Tovar Lodge

Bathroom in room 6441 at the El Tovar Lodge

Kachina Lodge

5 North Village Loop Drive
Grand Canyon, AZ 86023
(888) 297-2757
www.grandcanyonlodges.com

Kachina Lodge is located next door to the El Tovar Hotel on the canyon rim. This contemporary property was built in the 1960s, and the brick interior walls reflect the style of the era.

There's no front desk for this property, so guests check-in at the El Tovar Hotel. Kachina Lodge features two wheelchair-accessible rooms, both of which have tub/shower combinations.

Room 6318 features a wide doorway, a lowered peephole, low-pile carpet and good pathway access. It's furnished with a 26-inch high king-sized bed, an easy chair, a desk and a chair, and a chest of drawers. The bathroom has a tub/shower combination with a hand-held showerhead, grab bars and a portable shower chair. The toilet grab bars are located on the back and right walls (as seated). Other access features include a roll-under sink and a lowered mirror.

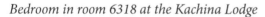

Bedroom in room 6318 at the Kachina Lodge

Bathroom in room 6318 at the Kachina Lodge

Bedroom in room 6320 at the Kachina Lodge

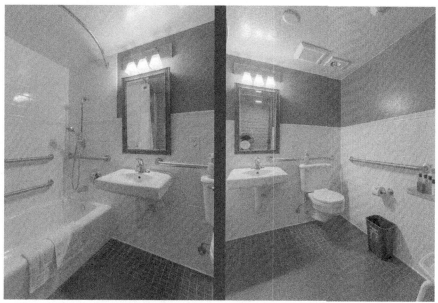

Bathroom in room 6320 at the Kachina Lodge

Room 6320 features the same basic access features as room 6318. It's furnished with a 26-inch high queen-sized bed with wheelchair access on the right side (as you face it). It has the same bathroom configuration as room 6318, except that the toilet grab bars are located on the back and left walls (as seated).

Both accessible rooms also include electric drapery controls and a refrigerator.

As noted earlier, Kachina Lodge is also the only property in the park with an elevator, so it's a good choice for slow walkers who want a standard room on an upper floor.

Thunderbird Lodge

7 North Village Loop Drive
Grand Canyon, AZ 86023
(888) 297-2757
www.grandcanyonlodges.com

Located next door to Kachina Lodge, Thunderbird Lodge is identical in style and ambiance. This property has three wheelchair-accessible rooms, which are equipped with a roll-in shower or a tub/shower combination. It's also the only property in the park that has wheelchair-accessible rooms with canyon views.

Bedroom in room 6213 at the Thunderbird Lodge

Bathroom in room 6213 at the Thunderbird Lodge

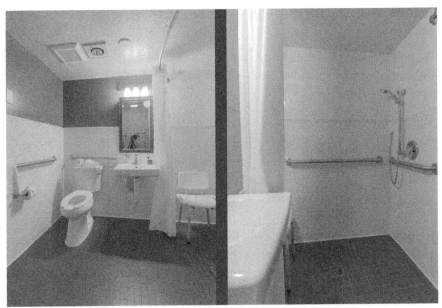

Like the Kachina Lodge, there's no front desk at the Thunderbird Lodge, so guests check-in at the Bright Angel Lodge, which is located next door. Accessible parking is located near the main entrance to Bright Angel Lodge, with ramp access up to the automatic front doors, and a barrier-free pathway over to the front desk. There is also level access to Bright Angel Lodge from the canyon side.

There's level access to room 6213 at Thunderbird Lodge, which features wide doorways, a lowered peephole, low-pile carpet and good pathway access. It's furnished with two 26-inch high queen-sized beds with an access aisle between them, a chest of drawers, and a desk and a chair.

There's is a sliding door to the bathroom, which is equipped with a roll-in shower with a hand-held showerhead, grab bars and a portable shower chair. The toilet grab bars are located on the back and right walls (as seated), and the bathroom also has a roll-under sink.

Room 6211 has the same access features and bed configuration as room 6213, except that it also has a second door which opens out to the canyon.

Room 6209 also has the same access features and bed configuration as room 6213, except that the bathroom is equipped with a tub/shower combination.

All three accessible rooms also include electric drapery controls and a refrigerator.

Maswik Lodge

202 South Village Loop Drive
Grand Canyon, AZ 86023
(888) 297-2757
www.grandcanyonlodges.com

Maswik Lodge is a motel-style property, with parking located right outside the rooms. The property is spread out between buildings dotted throughout a pine forest. Formerly it was divided into a north and south section, but the older south section has been demolished and plans are underway to construct a new lodge complex. The new addition, which will include accessible rooms, is scheduled to be completed in 2021.

The north section has 10 wheelchair-accessible rooms which are equipped with a roll-in shower or a tub/shower combination. Accessible parking is located near the main lobby, with level access to the entrance, and a barrier-free pathway over to the front desk.

Room 6761 is located near the main lodge in the Cliffrose Building. There's

Bedroom in room 6761 at the Maswik Lodge

Bathroom in room 6761 at the Maswik Lodge

accessible parking in front, with level access to the room. Other access features include wide doorways, a lowered peephole, lever handles and a lowered closet rod. It's furnished with two 23-inch high queen-sized beds, with wheelchair access between them, a chest of drawers, a table with two chairs, and a refrigerator. It also has a sliding glass door, with level access out to a small patio area.

The bathroom has a roll-in shower with grab bars, a hand-held showerhead and a fold-down shower bench. The toilet grab bars are located on the back and left walls (as seated), and the bathroom also has a roll-under sink and a lowered mirror.

Room 6892, which is located in the Spruce Building has the same general access features and bed configuration as room 6761, except that the bathroom is equipped with a tub/shower combination, with grab bars and a portable shower chair. The toilet grab bar configuration and sink location are the same as in room 6761.

Room 6742 is located in the Aspen Building, close to the main lodge. It has the same access features and bed configuration as room 6761, except that the bathroom is equipped with a tub/shower combination with grab bars, a hand-held showerhead and a portable shower chair. The toilet grab bars are located on the back and right walls (as seated), and a large roll-under sink is located just outside of the bathroom. This room also has a sliding glass door that leads out to a patio; however there is one step down to it.

Bedroom in room 6892 at the Maswik Lodge

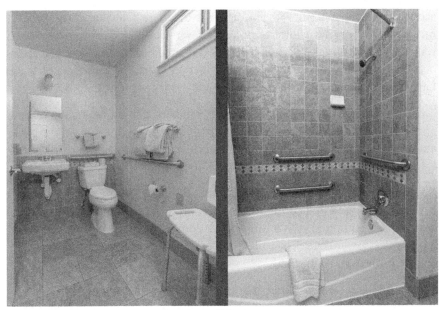
Bathroom in room 6892 at the Maswik Lodge

Additionally, there's barrier-free access to all the public areas of Maswik Lodge, including the restaurants, gift shop and lobby area. Accessible restrooms are located across from the front desk.

Yavapai Lodge

11 Yavapai Lodge Road
Grand Canyon, AZ
(877) 404-4611
www.visitgrandcanyon.com

Located in a pine forest near Market Plaza, Yavapai Lodge features eight wheelchair-accessible rooms equipped with a roll-in shower or a tub/shower combination. The main lodge building is located across the parking lot from Canyon Village Market & Deli. There's accessible parking near the building, with an accessible pathway to the front door and level access to the lobby. Inside there's plenty of room to navigate a wheelchair over to the front desk. The park shuttle bus also stops directly in front of the main lodge building.

The accessible rooms are located a short drive away, in the Yavapai East section of the property. Accessible parking is located in front of the buildings, with barrier-free access over to individual rooms.

Room 7426 features a key-operated automatic door, that can also be operated with a closed fist from the inside of the room. Other access features include

Bedroom in room 7426 at the Yavapai Lodge

wide doorways, a lowered peephole, low-pile carpet, a lowered closet rod and good pathway access. The room is furnished with a 30-inch high king-sized bed with wheelchair access on both sides, two night stands, an easy chair, a chest of drawers, a desk with a chair and a refrigerator.

A pocket door leads to the bathroom, which is equipped with a roll-in shower with grab bars, a hand-held showerhead and a portable shower chair. The toilet grab bars are located on the back and right walls (as seated), and the bathroom also includes a roll-under sink.

Bathroom in room 7426 at the Yavapai Lodge

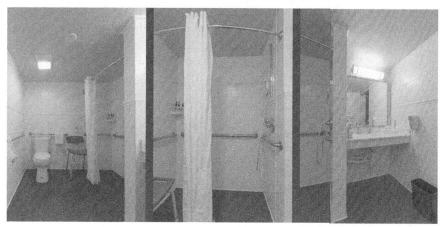

Bedroom in room 7304 at the Yavapai Lodge

Room 7304 and room 7420 include the same basic access features as room 7426, but they are furnished with two 30-inch high queen-sized beds with wheelchair access between them. The bathroom is equipped with a roll-in shower, with grab bars, a hand-held showerhead and a portable shower bench. The toilet grab bars are located on the back and left walls (as seated), and the bathroom also includes a roll-under sink.

Room 7310 has the same access features and bed configuration as room 7304, but it's a mirror image, so the toilet grab bars are located on the back and right walls (as seated).

Room 7260 has the same basic access features as room 7426. It's furnished with two 30-inch high queen-sized beds, with wheelchair access between them. The bathroom is equipped with a tub/shower combination with grab bars, a hand-held showerhead and a portable shower bench. The toilet grab bars are located on the back and right walls (as seated), and the bathroom also includes a roll-under sink.

Room 7370 is a mirror image of room 7260. It offers the same access features and bed configuration of room 7260, but the toilet grab bars are located on the back and left walls (as seated).

Room 7254 includes the same basic access features as room 7426. It is furnished with two 30-inch high queen-sized beds with an access aisle

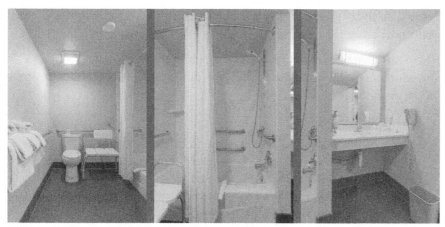

Bathroom in room 7260 at the Yavapai Lodge

between them, and includes a bathroom that is equipped with a tub/shower combination, with grab bars, a hand-held showerhead and a portable shower bench. It also has a toilet with grab bars and a roll-under sink.

Room 7376 contains the same basic access features as room 7426. It's furnished with a 30-inch high king-sized bed, with wheelchair access on the left side (as you face it). It also includes a small 18-inch high sleeper sofa. The bathroom is equipped with a tub/shower combination with grab bars, a hand-held showerhead and a portable shower chair. The toilet grab bars are

Bedroom in room 7376 at the Yavapai Lodge

located on the back and right walls (as seated), and the bathroom also has a roll-under sink.

There's also barrier-free access to all the public areas of Yavapai Lodge, including the restaurant, bar, coffee shop, gift shop and accessible restrooms in the main lodge building.

Mather Campground

Located south of Trailer Village off of Market Plaza Road, Mather Campground offers a good selection of wheelchair-accessible campsites. Accessible parking is available near the camper registration desk, with level access over to the check-in window. Lowered pay phones are also located near the camper registration desk.

All of the accessible campsites have parking on a paved level area, an accessible picnic table, a raised grill and a level tent site. Additionally, they are all located close to a restroom equipped with an accessible stall and a roll-under sink. It should also be noted that this is a fairly level campground, so many of the standard campsites may also work for wheelchair-users and slow walkers. As an added bonus, all of the campsites have accessible picnic tables. The campsites are separated by a pine forest, and it's not unusual to see deer and elk grazing there in the mornings.

Campsites 20, 23, 51, 53 in the Aspen Loop, 131 in the Juniper Loop, and 278 and 303 in the Pine Loop are designated as wheelchair-accessible on www.recreation.gov. Campsites 17 in the Aspen Loop, and 280, 316 and 318 in the Pine Loop have the same access features but they are not designated as wheelchair-accessible on the reservation website.

Campsite reservations may be made up to six months in advance at www.recreation.gov or (877) 444-6777. Reservations for accessible sites may require proof of disability upon arrival. If nobody has a need for an accessible site, able-bodied campers may be asked to move to a non-accessible site if a qualified person with a disability has a need for the accessible site. Accessible sites may not be reserved by able-bodied campers unless they are the only sites left at the time of reservation.

The campground amphitheater (campfire circle) is located at the end of a rocky path near the Sage Loop; however it's not wheelchair accessible.

Mather Campground is open all year.

Trailer Village

Trailer Village is the only campground in the park that offers full RV hookups. Although there are no designated wheelchair-accessible sites there, most of the spaces are level and they may work for some wheelchair-users and slow walkers. There are no accessible restrooms in this campground, and the office has steps in the front. Trailer Village is operated by Delaware North, and campsites can be reserved at www.visitgrandcanyon.com or (877) 404-4611. Trailer Village is open year-round.

Dining

El Tovar Dining Room

The elegant El Tovar Dining Room features ramp access from the hotel lobby and plenty of room to navigate a wheelchair. The restaurant is open for breakfast, lunch and dinner; and the menu features traditional offerings with a definite Southwestern flair. Customer favorites include Navajo Tacos, Salmon Tostadas and their signature Prime Rib Hash. Breakfast is a real treat, with perfectly cooked-to-order eggs and all the trimmings. Additionally this restaurant employs the most experienced servers in the park, so dining there is a top-drawer affair. Dinner reservations are highly recommended, and hotel guests can make them 90 days in advance, while others can make them 30 days in advance. Reservations can be made by calling (928) 638- 2631 ext. 6432, e-mailing gcsrdining@xanterra.com, or online at www.grandcanyonlodges.com. And while jackets are not required in this fine dining establishment, guests are asked to dress appropriately and refrain from wearing shorts and flip flops.

El Tovar Lounge

There's barrier-free access to the El Tovar Lounge, which offers light meals and adult beverages. The menu features house favorites such as Mozzarella Roulade and Crab-cake Sliders. Beer, wine and mixed drinks are also available. This quiet hideaway makes an excellent before of after dinner stop.

Arizona Room

Located on the canyon rim between the Bright Angel Lodge and Thunderbird Lodge, the Arizona Room is open for lunch and dinner. The main entrance has steps down into the restaurant, but there is a level accessible entrance on the canyon side. This traditional steakhouse features everything from BBQ ribs and Southwestern chicken and fish entrees, to a nice selection of aged, hand-cut steaks, as well as a sprinkling of

Southwestern treats like green chile tamales. Sandwiches and grill items are also available at lunch. And you just can't beat the panoramic canyon view. Dinner reservations are suggested at this popular eatery. They can be made 30 days in advance by calling (928) 638- 2631 ext. 6432, e-mailing gcsrdining@xanterra.com, or online at www.grandcanyonlodges.com.

Harvey House Cafe

This casual coffee shop is located in the Bright Angel Lodge, with ramp access up from the lobby area. It's open for breakfast, lunch and dinner. Burgers, fajitas and sandwiches are the mainstay of this family-style restaurant, but it also offers chicken, pasta, beef and Southwestern entrees. It's a good place for a quick bite, and an excellent choice for parents with kids in tow. As an added bonus, this eatery also features some historic Harvey House favorites on the menu.

Canyon Coffee House

There's barrier-free access to this coffee house at Bright Angel Lodge, where coffee, espresso, cappuccino, pastries and fresh fruit are available in the morning. If you want a quick and light breakfast, this is the place for you.

Bright Angel Fountain

There's level access to this fountain from the canyon side of Bright Angel Lodge. Open seasonally, this snack stand features sandwiches, hot dogs, pastries, fresh fruit and a variety of beverages. It's a good place to stop for a light snack or a grab-and-go lunch.

Maswik Food Court

The Maswik Food Court features several stations that offer plated lunches and dinners, salads and sandwiches to go, cooked-to-order breakfast dishes, and light snacks. There is level access to the food court from the front lobby, with ample room to navigate a wheelchair in the serving and seating areas. Healthy options are available at most stations, including fruit, oatmeal, cereal, gluten-free buns and veggie burgers. It's a good choice for families.

Maswik Pizza Pub

The Maswik Pizza Pub is located next door to the Maswik Food Court, and it features level access with plenty of room to maneuver a wheelchair. It's the place to go for pizza in the park, and the menu also includes wings, salad, beer, wine and soft drinks. Additionally the pub has four televisions for optimum sports coverage, so you can keep up with your favorite team while you're in the park.

Yavapai Lodge Restaurant

Open for breakfast, lunch and dinner the Yavapai Lodge Restaurant features level access from the lobby, and plenty of room to maneuver a wheelchair around the tables. Guests order from automated kiosks and pick up their food at the counter. A breakfast buffet as well as ala carte items are available in the morning; while the restaurant offers a good selection of soups, salads, sandwiches and hearty entrees the rest of the day. Entree offerings include everything from beef brisket and cowboy steak to lighter vegetarian options. Beer and wine are also available.

Yavapai Tavern

Located around the corner from the Yavapai Lodge Restaurant, the Yavapai Tavern is open in the late afternoon and early evening. This casual restaurant features ramp access, and also includes a family-friendly seating area for patrons with small kids. Menu offerings include a good selection of sandwiches, burgers, salads, appetizers and small plates. The restaurant also has a full bar.

Yavapai Coffee Shop

Located off the lobby of Yavapai Lodge, this snack counter features level access, with plenty of room to maneuver a wheelchair. It's the place to stop for coffee and a bagel for breakfast, or to grab a sandwich, wrap or salad to eat along the trail. As an added bonus, the menu also features a number of healthy selections.

Canyon Village Market & Deli

The Canyon Village Market & Deli is located at Market Plaza, across from Yavapai Lodge and next to the post office. There's accessible parking near the front door and level access to this large market which carries camping equipment, clothing and souvenirs as well as standard grocery fare. Customers can select from a large selection of fresh produce, hand-cut meats, and cooking staples to create their own meals; or stop by the deli for a freshly made sandwich or salad. Beer, wine and non-alcoholic beverages are also available. Accessible seating is located in the deli area and also in front of the market. Free Wi-Fi is available here, but the signal strength is usage dependent. Accessible restrooms are located on the side of the building, along a barrier-free pathway from the accessible parking area.

Mather Point Cafe

Located next to the Grand Canyon Visitor Center, the Mather Point Cafe is operated by the owners of Bright Angel Bicycle Rentals. There's level access to the front door of the building, and barrier-free access inside. Menu offerings include coffee and pastries, plus a variety of grab-and-go sandwiches and salads. Juices, sodas and energy drinks are also available. It's a good place to pick up lunch to enjoy along the trail.

Desert Dog Food Truck

New in 2018, the Desert Dog Food Truck can be found at popular stops along the South Rim. Access is dependent on the location, but in most cases the food truck is parked in a level area. From April to September the Desert Dog Food Truck offers standard hot dogs with a variety or toppings, as well as Bison Franks and Smoked Bison Bratwurst. Soft drinks, water and iced tea are also available.

Fuel Your Hike Cart

Also new in 2018 is the Fuel Your Hike Cart, which is located at popular trailheads along the South Rim. Like the Desert Dog Food Truck, access at the Fuel Your Hike Cart is dependent upon its placement, but many times it's parked in a level and accessible spot. Offerings include granola bars, jerky, cookies, drinks and other items to fuel your hikes. This cart is open from April to October.

Services

Mather Campground Showers & Laundry

The Mather Campground Showers & Laundry are located in the Camper Services Building, next to the camper registration area. Accessible parking is located near the building, with ramp access to the front door. Inside there's level access to the laundry area; however there are no wheelchair-accessible showers or toilet stalls in the shower area. Additionally, because of some tight corners and narrow pathways, the shower area is not wheelchair-accessible

North Country Clinic

(928) 638-2551

This medical clinic provides routine medical services to residents and visitors, and it also includes an urgent care center and a pharmacy. There's accessible parking in the adjacent lot, and also near the clinic entrance. There's level access to the building and barrier-free access inside. The clinic is located at the end of Clinic Road, which is off of Center Road, halfway between South Entrance Road and Village Loop Drive. The urgent care center is open seven days a week from Memorial Day to Labor Day, and on weekdays the rest of the year. The pharmacy and the medical clinic are open on weekdays year-round.

Library

The public library is located near the train depot, along the Greenway Trail. That said, the inaccessible back entrance faces the trail, and there isn't a level pathway to the accessible front entrance from that access point. It's best to take the Greenway Trail to Navajo Drive and follow that road until it dead-ends at the library. You can also drive if you have a vehicle; however the level lot is not striped. There's ramp access up to the library in the front, and although some areas of the building may be a bit tight for large wheelchairs it's mostly doable. Free Wi-Fi and public computers are available at the library.

Park Headquarters

Park Headquarters is located across the street from Market Plaza, and next door to the Shrine of the Ages. Although it's largely an administration building, there's free Wi-Fi access in the lobby and public computers in the research library. Accessible parking is available in front of the building, and there's level access over to the entrance. There's barrier-free access throughout the building, and accessible restrooms are located near the lobby.

Grand Canyon Railway Station

There's level access to the boarding area at the Grand Canyon Railway Station, where the Grand Canyon Railway arrives and departs each day. Although El Tovar Hotel is located directly behind the station, there's only stairway access to Grand Canyon Village via that route. Alternatively there is level access over the shuttle bus stop which takes visitors down to Bright Angel Lodge, which features ramp access in front and level access out to the canyon rim. The closest accessible restrooms are located at the Bright Angel Trailhead, between Bright Angel Lodge and Hermit Road.

Post Office

There's level access to the post office, which is located between the bank and Canyon Village Market & Deli in Market Plaza.

Bank

There's level access to the bank, which features a wheelchair-height ATM in front. It's located next to the post office in Market Plaza.

Desert View Drive

Elevation 7,500 feet

Although Desert View Drive is technically part of the South Rim, it can also be accessed from the East Entrance, which is located 30 miles west of Cameron, Arizona. Named after the historic Desert View Watchtower, Desert View Drive runs from the east park gate to South Entrance Road, with several canyon viewpoints along the way. This section of the park is a good choice for folks who want to ditch the Grand Canyon Village crowds, and enjoy a quieter slice of the canyon. Since there's no shuttle service to this area of the park, you have to have a car or join a Xanterra bus tour to explore Desert View Drive. There are no public facilities at the East Entrance station.

Attractions

Desert View Watchtower

Located at the end of Desert View Drive, near the East Entrance to the park, the iconic Desert View Watchtower is a must-see if you venture along this stretch of the road. Accessible parking is located near the accessible restrooms in the Desert View Watchtower parking lot. There is also a level drop-off area on the other side of the restrooms.

Desert View Watchtower

Desert View Watchtower is located about a quarter-mile from the parking area, down a paved trail. That said, the trail has a sustained 1:8 grade, with no level spots along the way. It's quite doable for power wheelchair and scooter-users, however, manual wheelchair-users may need a bit of assistance on the trek back up to the parking lot. The steepest section of the trail is from the Trading Post to the Desert View Watchtower; however you can also get a good view of the watchtower near the Trading Post, if you are unable to make the trek.

There is level access to the first-floor of the Desert View Watchtower; however the upper floors are only accessible by stairs. There is a small gift shop and a visitor center inside the watchtower, which was originally designed as a rest area by Mary Colter in 1932. Colter envisioned the structure as something that would blend in with the surrounding landscape, so the view of the watchtower is just as impressive as the view from inside it. There is also level access to the overlook in front of the watchtower, which affords some magnificent views of the Grand Canyon.

Tusayan Museum
The Tusayan Museum and pueblo site is located between Lipan Point and Moran Point, on the south side of the road. There are two accessible parking areas; one near the accessible vault toilet, and the other near the entrance to the museum. There is level access from both parking areas to the museum,

Tusayan Museum

which features exhibits about the ancestral pueblo people who inhabited the site 800 years ago. Although there is plenty of room to navigate a wheelchair through the museum, it can get a little crowded during peak season. Outside, a quarter-mile accessible trail winds around the former pueblo site, with interpretive signs along the way. About midway along the trail, a gravel trail branches off to the farm area; however this trail is not accessible due to the gravel surface and a steep grade. Still the paved interpretive trail is definitely worth a stop, and there are benches to stop and rest along the way.

There's also level access to a small shaded picnic area across from the museum, which has a few accessible tables. And since it's not marked as a picnic area on the park map, it's usually not crowded, and makes a nice lunch stop.

Navajo Point

Navajo Point, which is located just west of Desert View, is the highest overlook — at 7,461 feet — along Desert View Drive. The parking lot is paved and striped, but it lacks any accessible spaces. The curbs are approximately eight inches high, and since there are no curb-cuts, there's no accessible way to get out to the overlook. Additionally, the path out to the overlook is bumpy and has a few steps along the way, so it's not a good choice for wheelchair-users.

View from the Moran Point Overlook

Lipan Point

Lipan Point, which is located west of Navajo Point, has slightly better access; however, it's still not technically wheelchair-accessible. Like Navajo Point, there's no accessible parking, and you have to be able to navigate an eight-inch high curb to access the overlook. The path out to the overlook is uneven and bumpy, and there are a couple of steps along the way. The upside of this overlook is that if you pull into one or two prime parking spaces you will get a good windshield view of the Colorado River in the canyon below; however, the overlook itself is not accessible for most wheelchair-users.

Moran Point

Moving west on Desert View Drive, the next overlook is Moran Point. There is accessible parking, with curb-cut access up to an asphalt path which leads out to the overlook. The path on the right side of the parking lot is the accessible one, as the one on the left has a few steps along the way. The overlook offers a nice view of the Colorado River, and you can even spot Cape Royal on the North Rim, eight miles across the canyon. This overlook also offers a good example of the layered Paleozoic sedimentary rock that makes up the lion's share of the Grand Canyon.

View from the Grandview Point Overlook

Grandview Point

Grandview Point is the most popular stop along Desert View Drive, and it's also one of the more accessible overlooks. There's accessible parking, with curb-cut access to the paved path which leads out to the overlook. Along the way there are interpretive panels about the Last Chance Copper Claim, which was located 3,000 feet below the rim and operated from 1890 to 1907, and the Grand View Hotel which graced this site in the late 1800s. Grandview Point also offers sweeping panoramic views of the Grand Canyon, including several bends in the Colorado River. Accessible vault toilets are also located near the accessible parking spots.

Duck on a Rock Overlook

Located west of Grandview Point, this unmarked overlook is worth a stop for the canyon view. The parking lot is paved, and since there's no striped parking it's easy to parallel park an adapted van there. There's curb-cut access over to the viewpoint, which includes an interpretive panel about how early explorers named rock formations after human or animal forms. The formation in the distance apparently looked like a duck on a rock to the person who discovered it; however you may or may not see the resemblance. Still, the canyon view from the overlook is great, so at least make a quick stop there.

Duck on a Rock Overview

Picnic Areas

Desert Watchtower

There's level access to this shaded picnic area which is located near the parking lot. The ground around the picnic tables is covered in wood shavings and mulch, so it may present some navigational problems for wheelchair-users. That said, there are a few accessible tables located close to the entrance, so many folks may be able to manage the short roll. Accessible restrooms are located next door.

Buggeln

Buggeln is a picnic area that is located west of Moran Point. The tables are located in an uneven dirt area which requires at least one or two steps down, so it's not a good picnic choice for anybody with mobility issues. There is however an accessible vault toilet located next to an accessible parking space, so it makes a good rest stop.

Desert View Drive

There are several unnamed picnic areas near the west side of Desert View Drive, close to the turnoff to Yaki Point — at Mile Posts 243, 244 and 248 respectively. None of these small picnic areas have accessible parking; and the one near Mile Post 243 is the only one with a vault toilet. That said, even though it is an accessible model, there is a two-inch step up to it because of erosion. Additionally that picnic area is usually filled with cars, as it's a popular parking place for Yaki Point hikers. All of these picnic areas have standard tables on uneven dirt pads, so they are really not a good choice for wheelchair-users. Ironically, the most accessible picnic area along Desert View Drive — across from the Tusayan Museum — isn't even designated as a picnic area on the park map.

Lodging

Desert View Campground

Located near the East Entrance to the park, Desert View Campground is usually less crowded than Mather Campground, and it provides a peaceful camping experience a short drive away from Grand Canyon Village.

Campsite 9 is designated as an accessible site. It features paved parking, an accessible picnic table and grill, and a level tent area. It's located next to an accessible family restroom that includes a toilet with grab bars and a roll-under sink.

Additionally, all of the campsites feature paved parking, and many of them include an accessible picnic table and a level tent area. The main factor that sets the accessible site apart from the others is its proximity to the accessible restroom; so many of the standard campsites in this campground are also doable for wheelchair-users.

Desert View Campground does not accept reservations, and it is only available on a walk-in basis.

Desert View Campground is open from mid-May to mid-October.

Dining

Desert View Deli

There's level access to the Desert View Deli, which is located inside the Desert View General Store. The menu includes a variety of soups and salads, plus breakfast burritos and made-to-order sandwiches. There's plenty of room to maneuver a wheelchair in the adjacent seating area, which is furnished with tables and chairs.

Services

Desert View General Store

There's level access to the Desert View General Store, which is located across from the accessible restrooms. It features camping supplies, grocery items, beer, wine and souvenirs. There's also level access to the Desert View Deli from the store.

Trading Post

There's level access to the Trading Post, which is located between the Desert View General Store and Desert View Watchtower. Inside there's a small snack bar and gift shop. There are also a few standard picnic tables on the level front porch.

Gas Station

Located near the campground, this gas station offers 24-hour access with a debit or credit card. There's level access to the building through a 32-inch wide door, and accessible restrooms inside.

North Rim

The North Rim entrance station is about a four-hour drive from Las Vegas, 30 miles south of Jacob Lake on Highway 67. From there, it's another 14 miles out to the Grand Canyon Lodge North Rim, which is located on the edge of the canyon. Only 10% of the visitors to Grand Canyon National Park make it to the North Rim, so if you want a quieter national park experience this is the place for you. The facilities are not as developed on the North Rim as they are on the South Rim, so you'll definitely need a car to get around and enjoy the scenic drives and viewpoints. There is one accessible porta-potty on the left side as you enter the park at the entrance station; however the parking area is small and this facility should only be used in an emergency. There is another accessible porta-potty at a pullout along the road to the Grand Canyon Lodge North Rim.

Attractions

North Rim Visitor Center

The best place to begin your North Rim visit is at the North Rim Visitor Center, which is located near the end of the road, down the street from the lodge. There is ramp access up to the building, with accessible parking available in the adjacent lot. Inside, you'll find interpretive exhibits, maps, brochures and a bookstore. A ranger is on duty to field questions, and a variety of interpretive programs are held there. A loaner wheelchair is available on a first-come basis, and accessible restrooms are located behind the visitor center.

Scenic Drives

Point Imperial Scenic Drive

This 11-mile drive, which begins at the North Rim Visitor Center and runs out to Point Imperial, is a must-do on any North Rim visit. It's about a 20-minute drive from the visitor center, but it's just five minutes from the "Y" intersection along the main road; so it also makes a good stop on the longer Cape Royal Scenic Drive. Point Imperial is the highest point in the park, at 8,803 feet; and the overlook offers spectacular windshield views of Mt. Hayden and Marble Canyon.

There's accessible parking and curb-cut access up to the sidewalk at the overlook. Although the short trail out to Point Imperial is paved, it's not a good option for wheelchair-users and slow walkers, because of the steep grade and the steps down to the overlook. There are some great canyon views from the level sidewalk in the parking area though, so don't pass up this stop.

There's also curb-cut access to a shaded picnic area across from the accessible parking spaces. There are a few accessible tables in the level area under the trees, and accessible vault toilets are located nearby. It's a very pleasant — and accessible — picnic area.

Cape Royal Scenic Drive

The longer Cape Royal Scenic Drive also starts at the North Rim Visitor Center and travels past the Point Imperial turnoff, and continues on to Cape Royal. It's 32 miles (one-way) and can easily be combined with the Point Imperial Scenic Drive, for a longer excursion. It takes about 45 minutes to get out to Cape Royal, without any stops along the way. This drive offers panoramic views up, down and across the canyon, with scenic windshield views at numerous overlooks along the way. There are also a lot of curves along the route, and it's not recommended for vehicles over 30 feet. Additionally, it may be closed in inclement weather, especially when there are high winds. Still there are plenty of great canyon views in fair weather at these scenic overlooks along the way.

View from the Point Imperial Overlook

Vista Encantada

There's no accessible parking at this viewpoint, which offers some stunning canyon views; however there's plenty of room to parallel park an adapted van. There's level access over to the overlook along a paved pathway that parallels the parking area. There's also curb-cut access up to the small picnic area, which has a few standard tables in a level area under some trees.

Walhalla Overlook

There's accessible parking and curb-cut access out to this canyon overlook, where the Kayunga Anasazi once lived. There's also level access to a 200-foot hard-packed dirt trail across the street, that leads around the ruins of Walhalla Glades — which once served as a summer camp for the former inhabitants.

Roosevelt Point

There's no striped parking at this viewpoint, but it's possible to parallel park an adapted van next to the viewpoint. The trail out to Roosevelt Point is not wheelchair-accessible, due to a steep slope, steps, rocks and other tripping hazards. Still the view from the main overlook near the parking lot affords visitors a glimpse of the stunning red rock canyon walls dotted with a bright green pine forest.

View from Vista Encantada

Angels Window on Cape Royal

Cape Royal

Cape Royal — the end of the line — offers accessible parking, with curb-cut access to the trail out to the viewpoints. Accessible vault toilets are located across the gravel parking lot, but because of erosion there's a four-inch step up to them. The paved trail to the viewpoints is wide and fairly level, and features a number of interpretive plaques that detail the local flora and fauna. The views along the route are to-die-for, with a teaser glimpse of Angels Window just a short walk from the parking lot. The canyon views continue, and near the .4-mile mark the trail branches off to the left towards Angels Window. It's just a 300-foot stroll out to the accessible overlook, which offers a panoramic canyon view with the Colorado River in the distance. Plus there's a comfy bench perched on the rim, so you can sit and enjoy the scenery. Back on the main trail, it's just a short walk out to Cape Royal, which offers an equally impressive display of eye-popping canyon views.

Picnic Areas

North Rim Campground

A small picnic area is located across the main park road from the North Rim Campground. There are a few accessible tables in a level spot just off the first parking area across from the campground; however the more

Cape Royal Trail

accessible choice is the second parking area near Norton Court. This parking area has a hard-packed dirt surface, whereas the first parking area is covered in gravel. Still, the first one will work for some slow walkers. As an added bonus, these picnic tables offer some beautiful canyon views. You just couldn't ask for a better lunch backdrop.

Lodging

Grand Canyon Lodge North Rim

Bridle Path
North Rim, AZ 86052
(877) 386-4383
www.grandcanyonforever.com

The Grand Canyon Lodge North Rim consists of a main lodge building surrounded by rustic cabins dotted throughout a pine forest. There's accessible parking near the main lodge building with level access to the front door, and a barrier-free pathway over to the registration desk. It should be noted that visitors with an accessible parking placard can drive beyond the "no vehicle beyond this point" sign, and park in the accessible parking spots near the front door of the lodge. Porter service for luggage delivery, and guest transportation in golf carts to and from the cabins are also available.

View from the main lodge building at Grand Canyon Lodge North Rim

This property features wheelchair-accessible cabins equipped with either a tub/shower combination or a roll-in shower.

Cabin 356 is an accessible Western Cabin, which is located close to the accessible parking area behind the visitor center. There's ramp access up to the roomy front porch which includes two rustic rocking chairs. Access features include wide doorways, lever handles, a lowered closet rod and good pathway access. The cabin is furnished with a 26-inch high queen-sized bed with wheelchair access on the right side (as you face it), a table with two chairs, and a desk with a chair. It also includes a refrigerator and a gas fireplace.

The bathroom is equipped with a roll-in shower with grab bars, a hand-held showerhead and a portable shower bench. The toilet grab bars are located on the back and right walls (as seated), and the bathroom also has a roll-under sink. Other access features include a lowered hair dryer, tissue dispenser and robe hook.

Cabin 348 is located next door, and although it has the same basic access features and furnishings as cabin 356, it's a mirror image of that unit, so the toilet grab bars are located on the back and left walls (as seated).

Western Cabin 315 has the same basic access features as cabin 356, but it is located closer to the main lodge building. The closest accessible parking

Bedroom in Western Cabin 356 at Grand Canyon Lodge North Rim (view 1)

Bedroom in Western Cabin 356 at Grand Canyon Lodge North Rim (view 2)

Bathroom in Western Cabin 356 at Grand Canyon Lodge North Rim

area is in front of the main lodge, but there's also a barrier-free pathway from the accessible parking area near the visitor center. The cabin features a large front porch with two rocking chairs, and is furnished with a 26-inch high queen-sized bed with wheelchair access on the left side (as you face it), a table with two chairs, and a desk with a chair. It also includes a refrigerator and a gas fireplace.

The bathroom is equipped with a tub/shower combination with grab bars, a hand-held showerhead and a fold-down shower bench. The toilet grab bars are located on the back and right walls (as seated), and the bathroom also has a roll-under sink.

Cabin 317, which is located next to cabin 315, includes the same furnishings and access features; however since it's a mirror image of that unit, there's wheelchair access on the right side of the bed (as you face it), and the toilet grab bars are located on the back and left walls (as seated).

Cabin 83, which is an accessible Pioneer Cabin, features ramp access from the nearby accessible parking area, and includes the same basic access features as cabin 356. It's furnished with a 26-inch high twin bed with wheelchair access on the right side (as you face it), and a 26-inch high double bed with wheelchair access on the left side (as you face it). Other furnishings include a desk with a chair, and a refrigerator.

Exterior of Western Cabin 348 at Grand Canyon Lodge North Rim

Bedroom in Western Cabin 315 at Grand Canyon Lodge North Rim (view 1)

Bedroom in Western Cabin 315 at Grand Canyon Lodge North Rim (view 2)

Bathroom in Western Cabin 315 at Grand Canyon Lodge North Rim

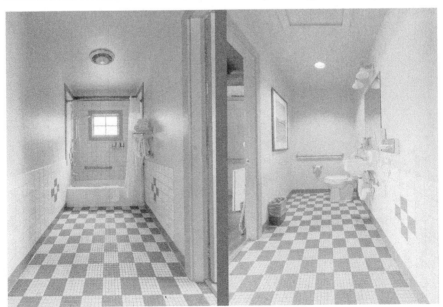

The bathroom is equipped with a roll-in shower with grab bars, a hand-held showerhead, and a fold-down shower bench. The toilet grab bars are located on the back and left walls (as seated), and the bathroom also has a roll-under sink.

Cabin 5, which is also an accessible Pioneer Cabin, has the same furnishings and access features as cabin 83, except that the toilet grab bars are located on the back and right walls (as seated). It's also closer to the main lodge, and accessible parking is available in front of the lodge with a level pathway to the room.

Cabin 29 is an accessible Frontier Cabin, which features wide doorways, lever handles and good pathway access. It's located just east of the main lodge building, and there's accessible parking in front of the lodge, with barrier-free access over a paved pathway to the cabin. There's ramp access to the cabin which is furnished with a 23-inch high double bed with wheelchair access on the left side (as you face it), and a 27-inch high twin bed with wheelchair access on the right side (as you face it), a desk with a chair, and a refrigerator. It's a very large room, with even enough space for a roll away bed.

The bathroom is equipped with a roll-in shower with grab bars, a hand-held showerhead and a fold-down shower bench. The toilet grab bars are located on the back and left walls (as seated), and the bathroom also has a roll-under sink. Other access features include a lowered robe hook and lowered towel bars.

Bedroom in Frontier Cabin 29 at Grand Canyon Lodge North Rim (view 1)

Bedroom in Frontier Cabin 29 at Grand Canyon Lodge North Rim (view 2)

Bathroom in Frontier Cabin 29 at Grand Canyon Lodge North Rim

Cabin 84 is also an accessible Frontier Cabin, and it includes the same basic access features as cabin 29. It's furnished with a 26-inch high twin bed, with wheelchair access on the right (as you face it), and a 26-inch high double bed, which can have wheelchair access on either side (it's located in an alcove and can be moved against either wall). The bathroom access features are the same as those in cabin 29, except that the toilet grab bars are located on the back and right walls (as seated).

There's good pathway access throughout the property, and new accessible cement walkways have been added over the years. There's also wheelchair access to all of the areas of the main lodge, but some facilities — like the gift shop and saloon — are accessed from a ramp in the back. Just follow the signs. Accessible restrooms are located next to the Deli in the Pines, with level access along the pathway from the front lobby. Additionally, there's lift access up to the auditorium in the front lobby, where ranger programs are presented in the evening.

One of the best features of this property is its location. Since it's perched on the canyon rim, it offers an excellent view. There's lift access from the front lobby to the Sun Room, which affords visitors a panoramic, yet sheltered, view of the canyon. From there, a level path leads out to the East terrace, which is the perfect place to enjoy the sunset in the great outdoors.

Exterior of Frontier Cabin 84 at Grand Canyon Lodge North Rim

Bedroom in Frontier Cabin 84 at Grand Canyon Lodge North Rim (view 1)

Bedroom in Frontier Cabin 84 at Grand Canyon Lodge North Rim (view 2)

Bathroom in Frontier Cabin 84 at Grand Canyon Lodge North Rim

North Rim Campground

Located near the General Store, this quiet campground features a number of accessible campsites, plus many others that may be doable for wheelers and slow walkers. Accessible parking is located near the camper registration kiosk, with level access over to the building.

There are three designated accessible campsites in the campground — 57, 60 and 76. They all have a paved parking area with level access to the site, an accessible picnic table on a paved pad, a level tent site and a raised grill. Additionally, they are all close to accessible bathrooms that are equipped with a stall with grab bars and a roll-under sink; however the restroom next to sites 57 and 60 has a slightly smaller stall.

There are also many campsites in this campground — like campsites 42 and 78 — that have all the access features of the above sites, except that the accessible picnic table is located on a level dirt pad. Many other sites have an accessible picnic table, and most of them have a raised grill. The terrain in the campsites is also fairly level.

Reservations for accessible campsites at the North Rim Campground can be made up to six months in advance at www.recreation.gov or (877) 444-6777. Reservations for accessible sites may require proof of disability upon arrival. If nobody has a need for an accessible site, able-bodied campers may be asked to move to a non-accessible site if a qualified person with a disability has a

Campsite 60 at the North Rim Campground

need for the accessible site. Accessible sites may not be reserved by able-bodied campers unless they are the only sites left at the time of reservation.

There's a level asphalt pathway to the campground amphitheater from the camper registration building, with plenty of room for wheelchairs in the front and on the sides. The amphitheater is also on fairly level ground.

The North Rim Campground is open from mid-May to mid-October.

Dining

Grand Canyon Lodge Dining Room

The Grand Canyon Lodge Dining room serves breakfast, lunch and dinner and features regional cuisine and 1930s-themed foods. There is lift access to the dining room, which is located inside the main lodge. A buffet is also available during breakfast and lunch. The breakfast buffet offers an assortment of hot and cold breakfast items, and the lunch buffet includes a salad bar and an assortment of pastas and sauces. An a la carte menu is also available at all meals. Dinner reservations are recommended, and they can be made by calling (928) 638-8560 or at www.grandcanyonforever.com.

Prime Rib Buffet

A prime rib buffet is held daily in the auditorium, from 4:30 P.M. to 6:30 P.M. The menu also includes chicken, pork and trout dishes with all the trimmings. There's lift access up to the auditorium from the lobby, and ample room to maneuver a wheelchair between the tables. Reservations are recommended, as seating is limited.

Roughrider Saloon and Coffee Shop

There's level access to the Roughrider Saloon and Coffee Shop, via a ramp in the back of the main lodge building. This eatery serves double duty, depending on the time of day. The Coffee Shop opens earlier than the Grand Canyon Lodge Dining Room, and offers breakfast burritos and assorted pastries, along with a variety of coffee drinks. Grab-and-go sandwiches for early risers are also available. The Coffee Shop closes in late morning, when the Roughrider Saloon opens, and serves pizza and assorted libations in the afternoon and evening.

Deli in the Pines

Open for lunch and dinner, the Deli in the Pines is located in the main lodge building, next to the restrooms. There is a step up from the parking area, but level access from the main lodge entrance. Offerings include sandwiches, salads, pizza and daily entree specials. It's also a good place to pick up a picnic lunch, or enjoy a scoop of ice cream after a long day.

Services

Showers

The public showers are located near the camper registration building in the North Rim Campground. There's level access to the shower house, which is equipped with a roll-in shower and an accessible stall on both the men's and women's sides. Accessible parking is located in front of the shower and laundry building.

Laundry

The self-service laundry is located next to the public showers. There's accessible parking in front with level access to the building, and plenty of room to maneuver a wheelchair around the machines. As an added bonus there are electrical outlets to recharge mobile devices next to a few tables out front.

Gas Station

The gas station is located near the turnoff to the campground. The automated pump is available 24-hours a day via credit or debit cards. There is one small step up to the office, but accessible restrooms are located on the side of the building, and they can be accessed from an exterior door. It should be noted that the prices at this gas station are quite reasonable, and competitive — and sometimes even lower — than those charged at the Jacob Lake gas station.

General Store
There's level access to the General Store, which is located near the North Rim Campground. Accessible parking and lowered pay phones are also available in front of the building. The store offers groceries, gifts, camping needs, snacks, wine and beer. There is also a small coffee shop with a small seating area in the back. There are tables and chairs on the front porch, and it's the only place on the North Rim that offers free public Wi-Fi.

Post Office
Located between the gift shop and the Roughrider Saloon and Coffee Shop in the main lodge building, the postal window features level access and offers customers the opportunity to get a "North Rim" postmark on their outgoing mail.

Nearby

Vermilion Cliffs Scenic Drive
The stretch of Highway 89A, which begins in Bitter Springs features stunning views of Echo Cliffs, Marble Canyon and the Vermilion Cliffs, as it climbs up to nearly 8,000 feet at the end point in Jacob Lake. Not only is this a very scenic drive, but it's also the most direct route to the North

Vermillion Cliffs viewed from the historic marker

Entrance from all points south. Plan a little extra time into your itinerary for several scenic stops along the way.

Vermilion Cliffs

Although there's no shortage of great windshield views of the Vermilion Cliffs on this drive, several viewpoints are also worth a stop along the way. Traveling north, watch for the "historic marker" sign on the east side of the road between Mile Post 557 and 558. Located a bit off the main road, there's level parking in a gravel lot, with level sidewalk access over to an interpretive plaque at this stop. Named by John Wesley Powell on his 1869 expedition, the multicolored shale and sandstone Vermilion Cliffs literally surround this viewpoint, and offer a prime photo op. Up the road, there's another scenic viewpoint near Mile Post 565; and don't miss the larger pullout on the west side of the road near Mile Post 568. Keep your eyes out for California Condors at the last stop, as they are frequently spotted in the area.

Navajo Bridge

Located near Mile Post 538, Navajo Bridge is a must-stop along the route. It's easy to spot, as the historic bridge parallels the current model along the main road. There's accessible parking near the old bridge — which was replaced with the current incarnation in 1995 — with level access to the accessible restrooms, visitor center and gift shop. There's also an accessible

Navajo Bridge with views of the Vermillion Cliffs

picnic table in the shaded picnic area near the historic bridge. Access is excellent at this site, and it's easy to roll across the 834 foot bridge which was constructed in 1928. And although bridge buffs will love this site, it also offers an impressive view of the canyon with the Colorado River below. The far side of the bridge is located on Navajo land, and it features a few trinket stands. Best of all, there's no charge to visit this site.

Grand Canyon National Park Resources

Grand Canyon National Park
(928) 638-7888
www.nps.gov/grca
www.facebook.com/GrandCanyonNationalPark
twitter.com/GrandCanyonNPS

Xanterra (in-park concessionaire)
(888) 297-2757
www.grandcanyonlodges.com
www.facebook.com/grandcanyonlodges

Delaware North (in-park concessionaire)
(877) 404-4611
www.visitgrandcanyon.com
www.facebook.com/visitgrandcanyon

Forever Resorts (in-park concessionaire)
(877) 386-4383
www.grandcanyonforever.com
www.facebook.com/GrandCanyonNorthRim

Grand Canyon West

J ust a three-hour drive from Las Vegas, Grand Canyon West is the newest development in the Grand Canyon. Located entirely on Hualapai land, it features the infamous skywalk, overnight lodging, food and beverage outlets and lots of spectacular views. And even though the facilities are located on tribal land and exempt from the Americans with Disabilities Act, the powers that be made sure that everything was built to be accessible, so everyone can enjoy the spectacular beauty at Grand Canyon West.

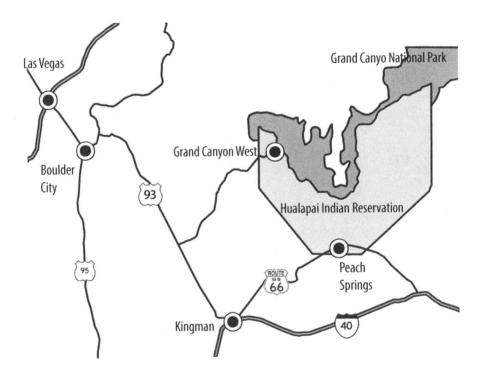

The Basics

Hours, Weather and Location

Grand Canyon West is open every day — including holidays — but unlike the national park, the gates are only open from 7:00 A.M. to 7:00 P.M. Advance reservations are not necessary; however plan accordingly as the last ticket is sold at 4:30 P.M. It should also be noted that Arizona is always on Mountain Standard Time as the state does not observe Daylight Saving Time.

In 2015 the last stretch of Diamond Bar Road was paved, so it's now a smooth drive through a Joshua Tree forest to Grand Canyon West for the final 21 miles of the journey. Grand Canyon West can be accessed from either Las Vegas or Kingman.

From Las Vegas, go south on US-93 for 72 miles, then turn left on Pierce Ferry Road. Follow Pierce Ferry Road for 28 miles, then turn right on Diamond Bar Road and continue on to the Main Terminal. The drive takes between two and three hours.

From Kingman, head north on Stockton Hill Road for 42 miles, and then turn right on Pierce Ferry Road. Follow Pierce Ferry Road for 7 miles, then turn right on Diamond Bar Road and continue on to the Main Terminal. The drive takes approximately one-and-a-half hours.

The weather at Grand Canyon West is very similar to the weather in Las Vegas. It's approximately 10 degrees warmer in the spring and summer, and 10 degrees cooler in the fall and winter. Rain is possible — even in the summer months — so it's a good idea to always pack along a light jacket.

Airports

The closest airport to Grand Canyon West with commercial service is Flagstaff Pulliam Airport (FLG), which is located about two hours away. It offers daily flights to Phoenix on American Airlines. Accessible van rentals are available in Flagstaff and at Phoenix Sky Harbor International Airport from Access Mobility of Arizona (www.wheelersvanrentals.com, 866-859-8880).

The larger Mc Carren International Airport (LAS) is about a two-and-a-half-hour drive from Grand Canyon West. This busy Las Vegas airport welcomes flights from around the world. Accessible van rentals in Las Vegas are available from Wheelers (wheelers-accessible-van.business.site, 866-859-8880) and Mobility Works (www.mobilityworks.com, 877-275-4915).

Shuttle Bus

Private vehicles are prohibited beyond the Main Terminal at Grand Canyon West. Park shuttle buses carry visitors from the Main Terminal to Eagle Point, Guano Point and Hualapai Ranch. The entire fleet is wheelchair-accessible, and these kneeling buses are equipped with ramps and tie-downs, and they can each accommodate up to four wheelchair-users. These hop-on hop-off buses run every 15 minutes, so visitors can spend as much time at each stop as they want.

Prices and Packages

Since Grand Canyon West is located on tribal land, national park passes are not valid there. Several packages are available, including the Hualapai Legacy Day Pass ($46.95), which includes admission and shuttle service to Eagle Point, Guano Point and Hualapai Ranch. The Legacy Skywalk Package ($66.90) includes the Hualapai Legacy Day Pass, plus admission to the Skywalk. The Legacy Gold Package ($76.86) includes the Hualapai Legacy Day Pass, admission to the Skywalk, and a meal at the viewpoint of your choice (except Sa' Nyu Wa Restaurant). A Legacy With Meal Package

Accessible shuttle bus at Grand Canyon West

($61.90), which includes the Legacy Day Pass, plus lunch at the viewpoint of your choice (except Sa' Nyu Wa Restaurant) is also available. All of the Grand Canyon West restaurants also accept cash. No outside food is allowed in the park.

Attractions

Main Terminal

The Main Terminal area is the first stop for Grand Canyon West visitors, where you can purchase admission tickets, use the restrooms or grab a bite to eat at the food truck. There's plenty of accessible parking near the terminal building, with level access from the adjacent parking lot. Inside there's barrier-free access to the gift shop, accessible restrooms and the ticket counter. The shuttle bus stop is located behind the main terminal, along a level pathway from the building.

Eagle Point

Eagle point is the first shuttle bus stop at Grand Canyon West. Named for the eagle rock formation on the canyon wall, Eagle Point is a sacred place to the Hualapai people. They believe that the spirit of the eagle delivers

Eagle Point at Grand Canyon West

prayers from people to the heavens. Out of respect, they have kept the canyon rim in pristine condition, so you won't find the requisite sidewalks and guard rails that are prolific on the South Rim. Although the parking area is covered in gravel, it's a level roll from the shuttle bus stop over to the canyon rim. It's a little bumpy, so some people may need assistance, but the view is great from just about every spot along the rim. Additionally, you'll find Hualapai ambassadors dressed in traditional clothing at all the sites. They are there to interact with visitors, answer questions, and share their culture and traditions, so don't be afraid to approach them.

Grand Canyon Skywalk

The highlight of Eagle Point is the Grand Canyon Skywalk, a u-shaped glass bridge that extends out over the canyon. There is ramp access up to the ticket line and level access to the adjacent locker area. Nothing is permitted out on the skywalk, so all purses, cameras, backpacks and bags must be left in the lockers. Ambulatory visitors are asked to wear disposable booties on the skywalk, but there are no restrictions for wheelchair-users. From the locker area, you can just roll right out to the skywalk, and get a bird's eye view of the canyon below. It's truly a once-in-a-lifetime experience, and you can take as much time on the skywalk as you want. And since cameras are prohibited on the skywalk, staff photographers are on hand to photograph visitors.

Grand Canyon Skywalk at Eagle Point

Amphitheater

There is a barrier-free pathway from the skywalk to the amphitheater, where tribal members from across the nation share traditional songs and dances. The dancers are dressed in their native regalia as they perform favorites such as the Hoop Dance, the Grass Dance and the Hualapai Bird Dance. The amphitheater is partially shaded, so it's also a good place to take a break from the sun.

Native American Village

The Native American Village, which is located near the amphitheater, features a collection of traditional dwellings hand crafted by tribal members. It includes a Navajo Hogan, a Havasupai Sweat Lodge, a Plains Tipi, a Hopi House, and a Hualapai Wikiup. There is an accessible path through the village, and visitors can roll right up to the dwellings and even have a look inside.

Native American Gift Shop

There's barrier-free access to this gift shop, which carries t-shirts and hats, as well as Hualapai-made jewelry and weavings.

Guano Point

Guano Point, which is the second shuttle bus stop, is the site of an

Visitors on the Grand Canyon Skywalk at Eagle Point

The Hopi House in the Native American Village at Grand Canyon West

abandoned bat guano mining venture. In 1958 U.S. Guano Corporation constructed a tramway system to extract the guano from a cave below the rim. Shortly after all the guano was extracted, an Air Force jet collided with the overhead cable system, so all that's left today are the towers. Today, you can get a great view of the canyon from the rim; however the walk out to the very tip of Guano Point is pretty rugged and not wheelchair-accessible.

Hualapai Market
There is level access over to the Hualapai Market, which is located next to the Guano Deli. The pathway is dirt and gravel, but it's doable for most people. Inside, there's plenty of room to roll around and browse through the wares of the Native American vendors.

Hualapai Ranch
Hualapai Ranch is the last shuttle bus stop; however, you can also drive there, because it's located outside the vehicle-free zone. It's about a mile from the Main Terminal, as you approach Grand Canyon West. It's also the site of the closest overnight accommodations.

Western Village
This re-creation of a western village features old time store fronts, horse stables, covered wagons and employees outfitted in western gear. Parking is

Entrance to Hualapai Ranch

available just outside the village in a large dirt parking area. The shuttle bus stops near a short dirt pathway that leads to the village. There is ramp access up to the boardwalk sidewalks inside the village, and most of the buildings have level access. You can also easily wheel around in the dirt in front of the store fronts, as there isn't any vehicle traffic through the town. Wranglers are on hand to teach visitors the finer points of roping, or show them how to toss a tomahawk. Wagon and horseback rides are also available, but they are not accessible.

Hualapai Ranch Gift Shop

There's barrier-free access to this gift shop, which carries everything from cowboy hats and belt buckles to Indian fry bread mix, rustic toys, and other Western merchandise.

Lodging

Hualapai Ranch Western Cabins

Quartermaster Point Road
Peach Springs, AZ 86434
(888) 868-9378
www.grandcanyonwest.com/hualapai-ranch.htm

Overnight lodging is available in the Hualapai Ranch Western Cabins, which are located past the Food Hall in a remote area of the village. Guests check-in at the telegraph office in the village. There is ramp access up to the boardwalk sidewalk, but there is a small step at the office entrance. The office can also be accessed through the gift shop next door, which has a level entry. There is no parking in front of the cabins, but guests can park there to drop off their luggage. Guest parking is in the remote dirt parking lot, which is not striped.

Cabin 19 is the accessible cabin. It features ramp access up to the front porch, a wide doorway and wood floors. It is furnished with a 27-inch high double bed with wheelchair-access on one side, and a 27-inch high twin bed in an alcove.

The bathroom has a wide pocket door and a full five-foot turning radius. It's equipped with a 35-inch deep roll-in shower with a 35-inch doorway. Other

Western cabin 19 at Haulapai Ranch

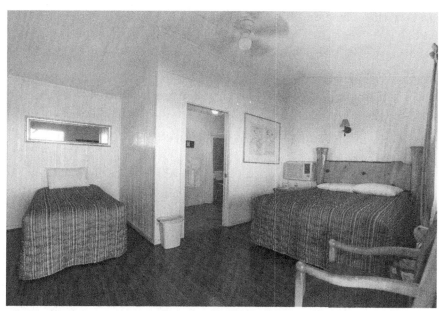

Sleeping area in western cabin 19 at Haulapai Ranch

Bathroom in western cabin 19 at Haulapai Ranch

 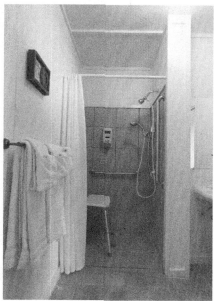

access features include a hand-held showerhead, shower grab bars and a portable shower chair. The toilet grab bars are located on the back and right walls (as seated), and a lowered mirror is located above the pedestal sink.

There is a large bench on the front porch, with plenty of room to maneuver a wheelchair around it. A fire circle is located nearby, where the resident cowboys make s'mores and entertain guests in the evenings.

Breakfast is included in the room rate. It is served in the Food Hall and consists of eggs, sausage, fruit, toast and hot or cold beverages. Additionally the folks at Hualapai Ranch are very accommodating, and they will do everything they can to make your stay more enjoyable.

A Legacy Day Pass must also be purchased in order to reserve a room at Hualapai Ranch.

View from western cabin 19 at Haulapai Ranch

Dining

Guano Deli

There is level access to this deli at Guano Point, which offers BBQ shredded beef, baked chicken and salads. There is level access to the covered outside seating area, and since it's located on the canyon rim, the view is excellent. Accessible restrooms are located nearby.

Sa' Nyu Wa

Perched above the Skywalk at Eagle Point, Sa' Nyu Wa is the newest culinary addition at Grand Canyon West. The menu features a good selection of soups, salads and sandwiches and also includes Asian entrees, traditional Hualapai tribal dishes and steaks and chops. Best of all, the restaurant's floor-to-ceiling windows offer patrons a panoramic view of the West Rim.

Skywalk Cafe

There is a level pathway from the skywalk over to the Skywalk cafe, which offers a nice selection of casual lunch fare. There's level access to the outside seating area, with accessible restrooms located nearby.

Hualapai Ranch Food Hall

The Hualapai Ranch Food Hall is located on the far end of the Western Village. There is a wide doorway at the entrance, and the one-inch threshold is easy to bump over. Inside, there's plenty of room to maneuver a wheelchair. Hot all-inclusive meals are served for lunch and dinner, and country entertainment is available throughout the day.

Grand Canyon West Resources

Grand Canyon West
(928) 769-2636
www.grandcanyonwest.com
www.facebook.com/grandcanyonwest

Lodging and Attractions
Along
Highway 64

Highway 64 links Williams with the South Rim of the Grand Canyon. The scenic drive offers some incredible windshield views along its 60-mile length; and although towns are limited along the route, Tusayan and Valle both offer a number of visitor services and lodging options.

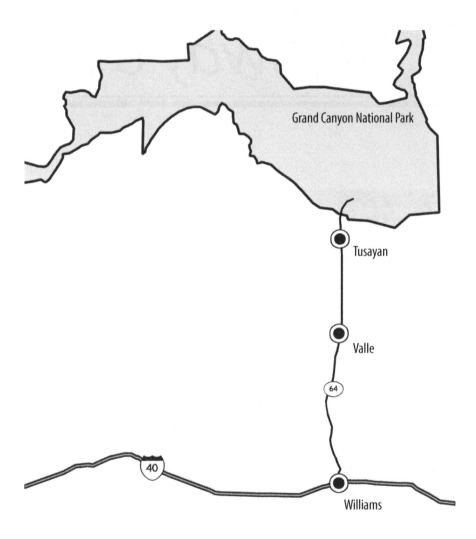

Tusayan

Elevation 6,612 feet

L ocated just seven miles from the South Rim, Tusayan is the closet town to Grand Canyon National Park. It's also the largest settlement along this stretch of Highway 64, and a popular overnight choice for South Rim visitors.

Attractions

National Geographic Grand Canyon Visitor Center

450 State Route 64
Grand Canyon (Tusayan), AZ 86023
(928) 638-2468
www.explorethecanyon.com

This comprehensive visitor center features a national park information desk, a National Geographic Store, a large cafeteria and an IMAX theater. Accessible parking is available near the front and back doors, with barrier-free access at both entrances. Accessible restrooms are located in the gift store — just follow the signs. There's a barrier-free pathway to all areas of the building, including Explorer's Cafe which serves pizza, sandwiches and Asian food, and offers box lunches to eat along the trail. There's plenty of room to maneuver a wheelchair around the National Geographic Gift Shop which has a good selection of souvenirs, books, DVDs and clothing. The six-story IMAX screen shows the movie *Grand Canyon; The Hidden Secrets* throughout the day; and although there's ramp access at the theater entrance, wheelchair-users must use the exit for level access to the wheelchair and companion seating area. If you cannot climb stairs or you disability is not apparent, inform the cashier that you need to use the wheelchair entrance when you purchase your ticket. Park passes are also available for purchase here.

Grand Canyon South Rim Chamber Visitor Center

469 State Route 64
Grand Canyon (Tusayan), AZ 86023
(844) 638-2901
www.grandcanyoncvb.org

Located across the street from the National Geographic Grand Canyon Visitor Center, this information station offers maps and brochures on attractions throughout the state. There's accessible parking in front, with level access to the building. Volunteers are also on-hand to field questions and make local reservations.

Grand Canyon Scenic Airlines

3555 Airport Road
Grand Canyon (Tusayan), AZ 86023
(800) 634-6801
www.scenic.com

Grand Canyon Scenic Airlines offers accessible flightseeing excursions over the Grand Canyon in fixed-wing aircraft from the Grand Canyon Airport in Tusayan. Accessible parking is located near the terminal with a barrier-free path to the front door. Inside, there's ample room to maneuver a wheelchair over to the counter, and through the adjacent gift shop.

This South Rim Airplane Tour is conducted in a Vistaliner aircraft, with large windows, so there's not a bad seat in the house. There are six stairs up to the aircraft door, but a portable ramp is available for anyone who can't manage the climb. Some manual wheelchair-users may need a bit of assistance with the slope of the ramp, but the crew is well versed in setting up the adjustable ramp as the owner's two sons are wheelchair-users.

Boarding ramp at Grand Canyon Scenic Airlines

There's a single seat with extra leg room by the aircraft door, and passengers must have enough trunk support to sit upright in the airplane seat. Wheelchairs and other mobility devices are stored at the terminal for this air-only tour. And although the crew is happy to set up the ramp, they are not allowed to physically assist with the boarding process or with transfers to the airplane seat.

The 45-minute South Rim Airplane Tour includes views of the Zuni Corridor, Imperial Point, the Confluence of the Colorado and Little Colorado Rivers, Kaibab National Forest and Kaibab Plateau.

Reservations for this accessible tour must be made in advance by phone, and the reservation staff is happy to field any access-related questions.

Papillon Aerial Sightseeing

3568 Airport Road
Grand Canyon (Tusayan), AZ 86023
www.Papillon.com
(888) 635-7272

Papillon Aerial Sightseeing offers several helicopter tour options for part-time wheelchair-users and slow walkers from the Grand Canyon Airport in Tusayan. Accessible parking is available near the terminal, with level access to the building and a barrier-free pathway over to the ticket counter.

Passengers must be able to board on their own, or with assistance from their party, and have enough trunk support to sit upright in the helicopter seat. The crew is not allowed to assist with boarding. Wheelchairs and other mobility devices can be stored at the terminal during these air-only tours.

The North Canyon Helicopter Tour features a loop route over the Colorado River to the North Rim. This 25-minute tour includes views of the North and South Rims, and Dragon Corridor, the widest and deepest section of the Grand Canyon. This tour is available in a standard helicopter or in the first-class Ecostar EC-130 which offers 180-degree canyon views.

The Imperial Helicopter Tour, which is conducted in the Eco Star EC-130, lasts for 45 minutes, and includes sweeping views of the canyon and Kaibab National Forest. The route takes guests by Point Imperial, over the North Rim, and then back through the canyon's central regions.

Reservations for all accessible tours must be made by phone, and the Papillon staff is happy to answer any questions about accessibility.

Lodging

Grand Hotel at the Grand Canyon

149 State Route 64
Grand Canyon (Tusayan), AZ 86023
(888) 634-7263
www.grandcanyongrandhotel.com

This three-diamond property, which is located just a mile from the South Entrance to Grand Canyon National Park, features seven accessible rooms equipped with either a roll-in shower or a tub/shower combination. Accessible parking is located near the entrance, with barrier-free access through the automatic door to the building. Inside, the spacious lobby is adorned with taxidermy mounts, and a circle of comfortable chairs that surround a massive fireplace. There's plenty of room to maneuver a wheelchair around the lobby, and over to the lowered registration desk.

Room 133, which is located on the first floor, features wide doorways, a lowered peephole, lever handles, a lowered clothing rod and good pathway access throughout the room. It's furnished with two 29-inch high queen-sized beds with wheelchair access between them, a night table, a desk with a chair, and a chest of drawers. It's also equipped with a microwave, a refrigerator and a Keurig coffee maker; and there's a roll-under sink just outside the bathroom.

The bathroom features a full five-foot turning radius and is outfitted with a roll-in shower with grab bars, a hand-held showerhead and a portable shower bench. The toilet grab bars are located on the back and left walls (as seated), and the bathroom also includes a lowered hook.

Room 229 features the same general access features and furnishings as room 133, except that it is furnished with a 29-inch high king-sized bed with wheelchair access on both sides. The bathroom is equipped with a tub/shower combination with grab bars and a hand-held showerhead. A portable shower chair is available upon request, and the toilet grab bars are located on the back and left walls (as seated). As with room 133, a roll-under sink is located just outside the bathroom.

Room 338 features wide doorways, lever handles and good pathway access. It's furnished with two 29-inch high queen-sized beds with an access aisle between them, a night table, a desk with a chair, and a chest of drawers. It also includes a microwave, a refrigerator, a Keurig coffee maker, and a roll-

Bedroom in room 133 at the Grand Hotel at the Grand Canyon

under sink that's located just outside the bathroom. There's a second door which leads out to a private balcony that's furnished with two chairs and a table. There's plenty of room for a wheelchair on the balcony, however some inside furniture might need to be moved in order for larger wheelchairs to clear the 30-inch pathway to the door.

The bathroom includes a tub/shower combination with grab bars and a hand-held showerhead. The toilet grab bars are located on the back and left walls (as seated), and a portable shower chair is available upon request.

Bathroom in room 133 at the Grand Hotel at the Grand Canyon

Bedroom in room 229 at the Grand Hotel at the Grand Canyon

The other accessible rooms at this property contain the same basic furnishings and access features as the rooms mentioned above. The bed and bathroom configurations for those rooms are listed below.

129 - One king-sized bed with a roll-in shower
229 & 304 - One king-sized bed with a tub/shower combination
233 & 333 - Two queen-sized beds with a tub/shower combination

There's elevator access to all three floors of this comfortable property,

Bathroom in room 229 at the Grand Hotel at the Grand Canyon

Bedroom in room 338 at the Grand Hotel at the Grand Canyon

and barrier-free access to the public areas, including the Canyon Star Steakhouse & Saloon, the gift shop, the fitness center and the business center. There's also level access to the lift-equipped pool and spa, which are located on the first floor. This full-featured hotel makes an excellent home base for any Grand Canyon visit.

Best Western Premier Grand Canyon Squire Inn

74 State Route 64
Grand Canyon (Tusayan), AZ 86023
(928) 638-2681
www.bestwestern.com

This 250-room property is conveniently located along Highway 64, just a short drive from the national park entrance. It features wheelchair-accessible rooms that are equipped with either a roll-in shower or a tub/shower combination, including several newly remodeled additions. There's accessible parking near the entrance to this three-diamond property, and barrier-free access through the automatic doors to the front lobby.

Room 4102 features wide doorways, a lowered peephole, low-pile carpet and good pathway access. It's furnished with two 28-inch high queen-sized beds with wheelchair access on all sides, a desk with a chair, a table and two chairs, a refrigerator and a microwave. A roll-under sink is also located just outside of the bathroom.

Bedroom in room 4102 at the Best Western Premier Grand Canyon Squire Inn

The bathroom is equipped with a roll-in shower with grab bars, a hand-held showerhead and a portable shower chair. The toilet grab bars are located on the back and left walls (as seated), and there's a second roll-under sink in the bathroom.

Room 4116 has the same basic furnishings and access features as room 4102, except that it has a king-sized bed with wheelchair access on both sides and a 13-inch high sleeper sofa. The bathroom is a mirror image of the

Bathroom in room 4102 at the Best Western Premier Grand Canyon Squire Inn

Bedroom in room 4116 at the Best Western Premier Grand Canyon Squire Inn

one in room 4102, so the toilet grab bars are located on the back and right walls (as seated).

Rooms 4104, 4105 and 4106 are the newest accessible additions to this property. They were added to the inventory in 2018, in the space that was formerly occupied by the hotel laundry. And to say that these rooms are spacious would be a huge understatement; as there's clearly room for a mountain of luggage and even the largest power wheelchair or scooter in them.

Bathroom in room 4116 at the Best Western Premier Grand Canyon Squire Inn

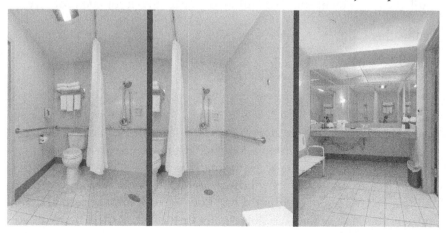

Bathroom in room 4104 at the Best Western Premier Grand Canyon Squire Inn

The rooms are all identical. Access features include wide doorways, a lowered peephole, laminate flooring, a lowered closet rod, and excellent pathway access. Each room is furnished with two 31-inch high queen sized beds with wheelchair access on all sides, a table and two chairs, and a wet bar with a refrigerator, a microwave and a Keurig coffee maker.

The equally spacious bathrooms are each equipped with a roll-in shower with grab bars, a hand-held showerhead and a fold-down shower bench. The toilet grab bars are located on the back and left walls (as seated), and each bathroom also has a roll-under sink.

There's elevator access to all floors of the property, and barrier-free access to the public areas including the restaurants, bar, business center and gift shop. Additionally, there's level access to the lift-equipped indoor pool and spa, as well as barrier-free access around the outdoor lift-equipped pool. It's a very comfortable, inviting and tastefully decorated property.

Red Feather Lodge

300 State Route 64
Grand Canyon (Tusayan), AZ 86023
(928) 638-2414
www.redfeatherlodge.com

Located near the IMAX theater on the main drag, the Red Feather Lodge has wheelchair-accessible rooms equipped with either a roll-in shower or a tub/shower combination. Accessible parking is available in front, with barrier-free access to the lobby through automatic doors. There's level access to the split-level building from the first floor in front, and the second floor in back; and most of the accessible rooms are located on these floors. There's

Bedroom in room 1122 at the Red Feather Lodge

also accessible parking near the back entrance.

Room 1122 features wide doorways, a lowered peephole, a lowered clothing rod, and good pathway access. It's furnished with two 26-inch high queen-sized beds with wheelchair access between them, two chairs, a desk and a chest of drawers. It also includes a refrigerator and a microwave.

The bathroom is equipped with a roll-in shower with grab bars, a hand-held showerhead, and a fold-down shower seat. There's also a portable

Bathroom in room 1122 at the Red Feather Lodge

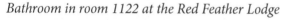

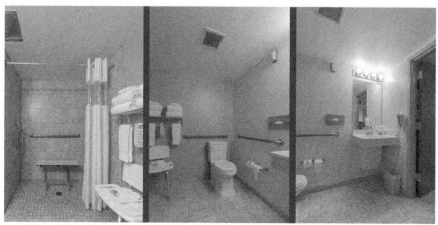

shower chair in the bathroom. The toilet grab bars are located on the back and left walls (as seated), and the bathroom also has a roll-under sink.

Room 1107 has the same basic access features and furnishings as room 1122, but the bathroom has a tub/shower combination with grab bars and a hand-held showerhead. The toilet grab bars are located on the back and left walls (as seated), and the bathroom also has a roll-under sink. A portable shower chair is available upon request.

There's barrier-free access to all the public areas of this property, including the lobby, business center, guest laundry and vending room. An accessible family restroom is located in the lobby, and there's barrier-free access out to the lift-equipped pool and spa in front. It's a very clean, comfortable and accessible Grand Canyon area lodging choice.

Bathroom in room 1107 at the Red Feather Lodge

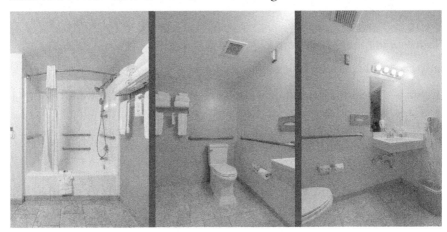

Valle

Elevation 5,993 feet

This small town is located midway between Winslow and Tusayan at the intersection of Highways 64 and 180. It's a good place to stop for gas, grab a bite to eat or even spend the night. And although Valle is seemingly in the middle of nowhere, it also boasts a few noteworthy attractions worth a stop on the way to or from the Grand Canyon.

Attractions

Planes of Fame Air Museum

755 Mustang Way
Williams (Valle), AZ 86046
(928) 635-1000
www.planesoffame.org

Located at the Valle Airport, across from the operations building, this vintage aircraft museum features over 40 military airplanes, many of which are flyable. There's accessible parking in front with barrier-free access over to the museum, The museum is located in a large hangar, which features level cement floors and barrier-free pathways to most of the exhibits. This

Inside the Planes of FameAir Museum

Messerschmitt BF-109 in the Planes of FameAir Museum

unique collection features everything from a Nazi Messerschmitt BF-109 to a Stearman PT-17. There's also display cases filled with aircraft parts, equipment, patches, models and even a bomb sight. Top it off with some airline memorabilia, a bevy of vintage photos, a B-17 instrument panel, and a mock-up of a Vietnam-era military command post, and you have a little something for everyone. There's also a bone yard out back, and even though the ground is covered in gravel, you can still get a good gander at it from the back door.

Lodging

Grand Canyon Inn

317 State Route 64
Williams (Valle), AZ 86046
(928) 635-9203
www.grandcanyoninn.com

This family-run property features 73 rooms in four different buildings, and it offers two wheelchair-accessible rooms with tub/shower combinations. There's accessible parking in front, with barrier-free access to the lobby building, and a level path over to the registration desk.

Room 119 is located a short drive away in Building C. There's accessible parking in the nearby lot and barrier-free access to the inside corridor of the building. Access features of the room include wide doorways, good pathway access, lever handles and low-pile carpet. It's furnished with two 25-inch high queen-sized beds with wheelchair access between them, a

Bedroom in room 119 at the Grand Canyon Inn

table with two chairs, a chest of drawers and a refrigerator. There's also a sink with an angled skirt just outside the bathroom.

The bathroom is equipped with a tub/shower combination with a diagonal grab bar and a portable shower bench. The toilet grab bars are located on the back and right walls (as seated).

Room 128 is located next door in the Building D. There's accessible parking near the door to the interior corridor, and a barrier-free pathway to the

Bathroom in room 119 at the Grand Canyon Inn

Bedroom in room 128 at the Grand Canyon Inn

room. Access features include wide doorways, a lowered peephole, lever handles, low-pile carpet and good pathway access. The room is furnished with two 25-inch high queen-sized beds with wheelchair access between them, a table with two chairs, a chest of drawers and a refrigerator. There's also a sink with an angled skirt located just outside the bathroom.

The bathroom is equipped with a tub/shower combination with a diagonal grab bar and a large shower chair. The bathroom grab bars are located on the back and left walls (as seated).

Bathroom in room 128 at the Grand Canyon Inn

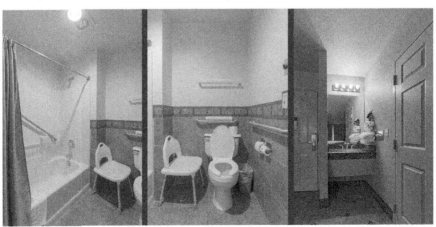

There's good access to the public areas of this property as well, including the bar, restaurant, and guest computer nook, which are located in the lobby building. There are also accessible restrooms near the registration desk. Additionally there's barrier-free access to the pool and spa area which is located next to Building D. And if you'd like to enjoy the desert air, tables and chairs are located in shaded shelters throughout the property.

And don't miss the classic cars that are parked around the Chevron gas station to the south of the main lobby building. There's also level access to the Valle Travel Stop next door, which carries snacks, drinks and souvenirs. Park passes are also available for purchase there.

Rocks & More, which is located on the north side of the lobby building, features accessible parking and a level entrance. Jewelry, rocks, crystals and a black light display room are featured on the inside, and there's even more rocks and a large offering of metal sculptures in the back lot. Even if you don't buy anything, stop by to see their museum-like collection of rocks. And don't miss the blue T-bird that's parked on the other side of the Mobile gas pump near the Rock Shop. It's truly a classic.

Grand Canyon Motel

317 State Route 64
Williams (Valle), AZ 86046
(928) 635-9203
www.grandcanyoninn.com

Door to room 70 at the Grand Canyon Motel

Bedroom in room 70 at the Grand Canyon Motel

This 28-room motel style property is located across the street from the Grand Canyon Inn; but it's owned by the same family that operates that property. There's no separate registration desk over at the motel, so guests check-in at the Grand Canyon Inn. The Grand Canyon Motel has one room that may work for some slow walkers.

There's ramp access up to room 70 (The Wyatt Earp Room) from the nearby gravel parking lot. Access features include wide doorways, level handles and laminate floors in this decidedly Western-themed room. It's

Bathroom in room 70 at the Grand Canyon Motel

furnished with two 27-inch high queen-sized beds with an access aisle between them, a night table, a desk and a chair, and an armoire.

The bathroom is equipped with a standard sink with a large counter, and it also includes a tub/shower combination with a diagonal grab bar. A portable shower chair is available upon request.

If you'd like a bite to eat, or want to wet your whistle, the facilities across the street at the Grand Canyon Inn are wheelchair-accessible. And don't miss their great collection of classic cars.

Highway 64 Resources

Grand Canyon South Rim Chamber & Visitors Bureau
(844) 638-2901
www.grandcanyoncvb.org

Route 66
and
Interstate 40
Corridor

A trip to the Grand Canyon is the quintessential road trip. That said, a journey to this popular national park doesn't have to be an out-and-back affair. Not only are there a bevy of attractions and natural areas in the towns that dot Interstate 40; but there are also spots where you can hop off the interstate and take a cruise along some of the few remaining stretches of Route 66. And if you'd like to stay a while, you can do that too.

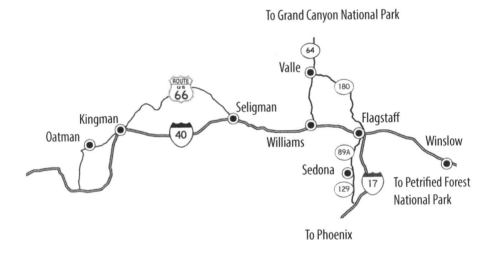

Kingman

Elevation 3,333 feet

Located about 2.5-hours from the South Rim, this Interstate 40 town makes a good stop for folks who approach the park from the west. The major attractions revolve around Route 66 and railroad history, while two intact sections of Route 66 allow visitors to experience a slice of the Mother Road. Add in some Route 66 themed diners, and you almost feel like you've stepped into another era.

Attractions

Kingman Visitor Center

120 W. Andy Devine
Kingman, AZ 86401
(928) 753-6106
www.gokingman.com

Located on the ground floor of the historic Powerhouse Building, which was constructed in 1907 to provide steam driven power to the area, the Kingman Visitor Center offers brochures and information about the

Kingman Visitor Center and Arizona Route 66 Museum in the

Powerhouse Building

Kingman area as well and the rest of the state. There's accessible parking in front with level access to the building, and accessible restrooms located around the corner. There's also an accessible cement table in front, with room for two wheelchairs, and a covered picnic shelter at the far side of the parking lot with tables with attached benches. A large gift shop is also located on the first floor, which offers a wide range of Route 66 gear, books, maps and other souvenirs. It's the perfect first stop for a Kingman or Route 66 visit.

Arizona Route 66 Museum

120 W. Andy Devine Avenue
Kingman, AZ 86401
(928) 753-9889

There's elevator access to this kitschy museum, which is located on the second floor of the Powerhouse Building. Admission is a very reasonable $4 ($3 for folks over 60), and the admission ticket is also good for the Electric Vehicle Museum, the Mohave Museum of History and Arts and the Bonelli House. And since there's no date on the admission tickets they're good for multiple visits to the covered attractions.

There's ramp access at the museum entrance, and even though there's a turnstile, there's also a gate for wheelchair-users. Inside there's plenty of room to maneuver a wheelchair around the exhibits that trace the history of

Kingman Route 66 Museum

Route 66 — which officially opened in 1926 — and its southwest precursor, the National Old Trails Highway.

Museum highlights include information on the Dust Bowl immigrants and the origin of the ubiquitous Burma shave signs. The Historic Route 66 Association of Arizona also has a room filled with exhibits and information about the era. Top it all off with a 1950 Studebaker, and some vintage storefronts, and you get a real feel for the era.

The museum continues downstairs, with an interesting film about the rise, fall and rebirth of the Mother Road. There are steps down to the theater seats, but there's wheelchair seating and benches in a level area in the back. The entrance to the Route 66 Electric Vehicle Museum is located just around the corner.

Route 66 Electric Vehicle Museum

120 W. Andy Devine Avenue
Kingman, AZ 86401
(928) 753-9889
www.hevf.org

Opened in 2014, this small but well curated attraction features an interesting collection of electric vehicles, the oldest of which dates back to 1909 — an Elwell-Parker baggage tug. There's level access to the museum

Route 66 Electric Vehicle Museum

from the adjacent Arizona Route 66 Museum, and plenty of room to maneuver a wheelchair around the exhibits.

The quirky collection includes everything from Willie Nelson's golf cart (complete with a beer tap), to the world's first all-electric hot rod. Educational institutions are represented too, with an Arizona State University electric Indy-style race car, and the rocket-like electric vehicle produced by the Ohio State University College of Engineering, which clocked in at 320 mph on the Bonneville Salt Flats. And don't miss the electric wheelchair that was built by a local from parts of a 1940s B17 bomber. Operated by the Historic Electric Vehicle Foundation, this fun museum illustrates the wide variety of electric vehicles produced throughout the ages.

Locomotive Park

310 W Beale Street
Kingman, AZ 86401
(928) 757-7919

Located across the street from the Powerhouse Building, Locomotive Park is home to historic steam engine #3759. Built in 1928, this locomotive pulled the train that traveled from Los Angeles to Kansas City, and took on water in Kingman. The locomotive was presented to the City of Kingman as a historical monument in 1957 by the Santa Fe Railway Company. The colorful caboose was added to the display in 1987.
Steam engine 3759 in Locomotive Park

There's good pathway access via a crosswalk from the Powerhouse Building to the park, but there's also accessible street parking on 1st Street at the far end of the small park. There's level access on a cement walkway around the locomotive, but there are several steps up to the locomotive itself. Still you can get a nice view of this historic piece of equipment from the park. There's also a picnic shelter with an accessible table near the accessible parking space.

Mohave Museum of History and Arts

400 W. Beale Street
Kingman, Arizona 86401
(928) 753-3195
www.mohavemuseum.org

This comprehensive museum presents a good overview of the history and heritage of the people of Mohave County. Accessible parking is located near the entrance and there's ramp access up to the front door. Accessible single-use restrooms are located across from the front desk, and the galleries all feature plenty of room for even the largest wheelchair or scooter. Highlights include exhibits about Route 66, the Native American people, mining history and local ranching. There's also an entire gallery devoted to Kingman's local celebrity, Andy Devine. Don't miss the outside exhibits which feature old farming implements, a walk-through gold mine,

Mohave Museum of History and Arts

a blacksmith's shop, and even a historic caboose. Even if you don't have time to tour the museum, stop by to admire the Route 66 mural that graces the front of the building.

Bonelli House

430 Spring Street
Kingman, AZ 86401
(928) 753-3195
www.mohavemuseum.org

Although this historic home isn't wheelchair-accessible, it may be doable for some slow walkers. And since it's included on the Arizona Route 66 Museum ticket, it's worth a look if you can manage one small step. Accessible street parking is available kitty-corner from the house. From there, a barrier-free path leads over to the home, and there's one step up to the former residence of George and Effie Bonelli. Although there are stairs up to the second story bedrooms of this 1915 house, there's level access to the first floor which contains Effie's bedroom (she had arthritis so she couldn't manage the stairs), a small bathroom, the kitchen, dining room and parlor. Some of the furnishings are original, and the kitchen even has Effie's old iron stove and hot water heater. Family mementos are scattered throughout the house, and there's always a docent on duty to answer questions and shed some light on the more personal aspects of the Bonelli family.

Bonelli House

Historic Downtown Walking Tour

While you're at the Kingman Visitor Center, be sure and pick up a Historic Downtown Walking Tour map, which contains a brief history of the town and describes 32 sites along the route. Technically the tour starts at the Mohave Museum of History and Arts, then travels to Metcalf Park, Locomotive Park and the Powerhouse Building, but you can do the tour in any order. The route from the Powerhouse Building down to the Kingman Railroad Depot is level, and the sidewalks all have pretty good curb-cuts. That said, the route on the north (Mr. D'z) side of the road is more accessible, as the south side stretch lacks a sidewalk near the depot. Additionally, the route up 4th Street to Beale is a bit steep, so you might want to drive to the different areas on the tour and then visit the nearby sites. The best part is — you can do as little or as much of the tour as you like, and you can even divide it up and do it on different days. It's a good way to learn about Kingman's history.

Kingman Railroad Depot

402 E. Andy Devine Avenue
Kingman, AZ 86401

This beautifully restored Santa Fe Depot is located about four blocks from the Powerhouse Building, on the corner of 4th Street and Andy Devine Avenue. There's accessible parking in the small lot, with ramp access up to the 1907 building There's also barrier-free access to the Amtrak waiting room, at the far end of the depot, which has accessible restrooms inside. Unfortunately

Kingman Railroad Depot

nothing remains of the Santa Fe Eating House — a Harvey House which was located across the street — but this depot is a must-see for railroad buffs. There's also an accessible picnic table near the access ramp, but it's not covered and it can get quite toasty, especially during the summer.

Railroad Museum

402 E. Andy Devine Avenue, Suite B
Kingman, AZ 86401
(928) 753-7995

Located next to the Amtrak waiting room at the historic Kingman Railroad Depot, this small museum is operated by the Whistle Stop Railroad Club. There's level access to the museum, which features three model railways — all of which are at eye level for wheelchair-users. Other artifacts include vintage railroad tools, photos, dinnerware and even an engine. The museum offers a good historic overview of Kingman and the railroad, and you can even see real trains pass by through the large picture window that overlooks the tracks. Don't miss the 1907 Fairbanks Scale, which was used to weigh freight at this depot.

Model train layout at the Railroad Museum

Lodging

Motel 6 Kingman West

424 W Beale Street
Kingman, AZ 86401
(928) 864-5705
www.motel6.com

Located down the street from the Mohave Museum of History and Arts, this budget motel features accessible rooms with roll-in showers or tub/shower combinations. There's a level drop-off area in front of the property, with barrier-free access to the lobby. There's also accessible parking in front of all the accessible guest rooms, with level access over to the rooms.

Room 101 features wide doorways, good pathway access, a lowered closet rod, and laminate floors for easy rolling. The spacious room is furnished with a 23-inch high open-frame queen-sized bed with wheelchair access on both sides, a desk, and a table with two chairs. It's also equipped with a refrigerator and a microwave.

The bathroom has a roll-in shower with grab bars, a hand-held showerhead and a fold-down shower bench. Two toilet grab bars (a vertical one and a horizontal one) are located on the right wall (as seated), and there's a

Bedroom in room 101 at Motel 6 Kingman West

Bathroom in room 101 at Motel 6 Kingman West

horizontal grab bar on the back wall as well. The bathroom also has a roll-under sink.

Bathroom in room 108 at Motel 6 Kingman West

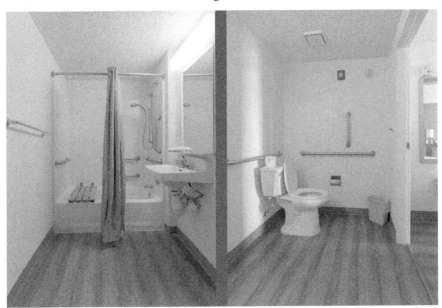

Room 108 features the same general access features as room 101, except that it's furnished with two 23-inch high open-frame queen-sized beds with wheelchair access between them. The bathroom is outfitted with a tub/shower combination with a fold-down slatted tub bench on the far end, grab bars and a hand-held showerhead. A vertical and a horizontal toilet grab bar are located on the left wall (as seated), and there's another grab bar on the back wall. A roll-under sink completes this nicely accessible bathroom.

And if you'd like to cool off, there's also a barrier-free pathway over to the lift-equipped pool, and good pathway access around the deck. All in all, this budget property has a great location — close to the Powerhouse Building — and the access features are really well done.

Best Western King's Inn & Suites

2930 E. Andy Devine Avenue
Kingman, AZ 86401
928 (753) 6101
www.bestwestern.com

This comfortable property, which is located near Interstate 40 at the east end of Andy Devine Avenue, makes an excellent home base for folks who want to explore the historic section of the Mother Road just east of the city. There's an accessible drop-off area in front of the property, with level access to the spacious lobby through an automatic door. The property has accessible rooms with roll-in showers or tub-shower combinations.

There's accessible parking in front of room 129, with barrier-free access to the front door. Access features include wide doorways, good pathway access, a lowered peephole and an accessible clothing rod. It's furnished with two 25-inch high queen-sized beds, with wheelchair access between them and on the left side (as you face them), a small sofa and easy chair, a desk and a chair, and a chest of drawers. The room also includes a refrigerator and a microwave.

The bathroom is equipped with a roll-in shower with grab bars, a hand-held showerhead and a portable shower chair. A horizontal and a diagonal toilet grab bar are located on the right wall (as seated), and there's also a grab bar on the back wall. A roll-under sink is located just outside the bathroom.

This property also has another accessible guest room with the same bathroom configuration, however it's furnished with a king-sized bed.

Room 130, has the same general access features and bed configuration as room 129; however the bathroom is equipped with a tub/shower

Bedroom in room 129 at Best Western King's Inn and Suites

Bathroom in room 129 at Best Western King's Inn and Suites

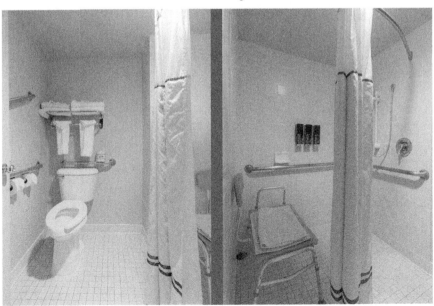

Bedroom in room 130 at Best Western King's Inn and Suites

combination with grab bars, a hand-held showerhead and a portable shower bench. The toilet is a mirror image of the one in room 129, with grab bars on the back and left walls (as seated). A roll-under sink is located just outside the bathroom.

There's good access to all the public areas including the lobby, the adjacent dining room (where a full breakfast is served), the guest laundry, and the lift-equipped pool. And even though all of the accessible guest rooms are located on the ground floor, there's also elevator access to all levels of the property.

Bathroom in room 130 at Best Western King's Inn and Suites

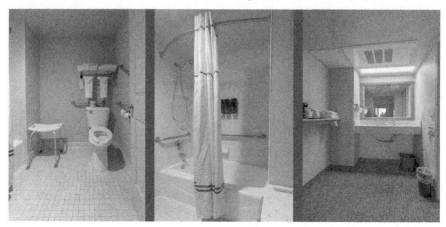

Marriot SpringHill Suites

3101 E. Andy Devine Avenue
Kingman, AZ 86401
(928) 753-8766
www.marriott.com

This upscale property offers accessible rooms with roll-in showers or tub/shower combinations; and it's conveniently located near Interstate 40 on the east side of town. Accessible parking is available near the entrance, with level access to the lobby through an automatic door. There's barrier-free access over to the front desk, and elevator access to all floors.

Room 309 features wide doorways, good pathway access and a lowered peephole. The living area is furnished with a 19-inch high trundle sofa (which includes a 10-inch high pull-out twin trundle bed), a coffee table, desk, refrigerator and a microwave. The adjacent bedroom includes a 27-inch high open-frame king-sized bed with wheelchair access on both sides.

The bathroom is divided into two rooms, and each area is accessed through a separate sliding door. One room has a tub/shower combination with grab bars, a hand-held showerhead and a fold-down slatted bench at the far end. The other room has a toilet with grab bars on the back and right walls (as seated). Both bathroom areas also have a large roll-under sink.
Bedroom in room 309 at Marriot SpringHill Suites

Living space in room 309 at Marriot SpringHill Suites

Room 410 includes the same basic access features as room 309, but it's furnished with two queen-sized beds. It's also a mirror image of room 309, so the toilet grab bars are located on the back and left walls (as seated).

Room 209 has the same basic access features and bed configuration as room 309, except that the bathroom is equipped with a roll-in shower with grab bars, a hand-held showerhead and a fold-down shower bench.

All of the accessible rooms also have a connecting room next door.

Bathroom in room 309 at Marriot SpringHill Suites

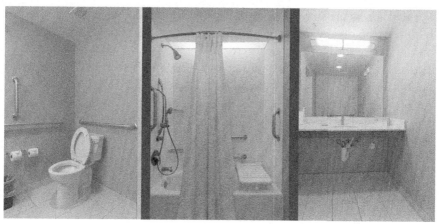

Bathroom in room 209 at Marriot SpringHill Suites

There's good access to all the public areas of the property including the business center, fitness room, meeting room and guest laundry. The property also includes an indoor lift-equipped pool. There's barrier-free access to the breakfast area, where a Continental breakfast is served every morning, and level access out to the adjacent patio area which features a pleasant fountain surrounded by tables and chairs. It's the perfect place to relax after a busy day of sightseeing, or to enjoy a quiet cup of coffee in the morning.

Dining

Mr. D'z Route 66 Diner

105 E. Andy Devine Avenue
Kingman, AZ 86401
(928) 718-0066
www.facebook.com/Mr-Dz-Route-66-Diner-115856938432156/

Located across the street from the Powerhouse Building, Mr. D'z is a required stop on any Route 66 adventure. Accessible parking is located on the side of the building, and across 1st Street near Locomotive Park. There's level access to the restaurant, and although there are a number of booths inside, there are also several tables that are wheelchair-accessible. Additional accessible seating is available at wood tables on the front patio. The single-use restrooms are large enough for wheelchairs, however the doorways are narrow and the toilets lack grab bars. This vintage diner is open for breakfast, lunch and dinner, and the menu features a selection of hearty breakfast dishes, a large burger menu, and a good variety of soups, salads and daily specials. And of course sundaes, malts, milk shakes and other ice cream confections are also available. Even if you don't go in, stop

Mr. D'z Route 66 Diner

by to see the incredibly cute Little Miss DD, a colorful little vehicle complete with eyelashes, that's parked in front of the diner.

Rutherford's 66 Family Diner

2011 E. Andy Devine Avenue
Kingman, AZ 86401
(928) 377-1660
www.facebook.com/Rutherfords-66-Family-Diner-155931257776855

This classic Route 66 diner is easy to spot — just look for the collection of gas pumps and other Mother Road memorabilia in front. Accessible parking is located near the front door, with level access over to the entrance. There's booth, table and counter seating inside, with room to maneuver a wheelchair around the tables. Some booths also have removable chairs on one side. The single-use restrooms have a toilet with grab bars in a 36-inch wide alcove; and although the doorways are wide, folks with larger wheelchairs may have problems with the tight approach. The diner is open for breakfast, lunch and dinner, and the menu is filled with breakfast favorites, soups, salads, sandwiches and hearty entrees. And even though some portions are quite large, there are also choices for folks with smaller appetites.

Rutherford's 66 Family Diner

Calico's

418 W. Beale Street
Kingman, AZ 86401
(928) 753-5005
www.calicosrestaurant.com

This family restaurant is just a short walk across the parking lot from Motel 6, so it makes an excellent breakfast or dinner stop if you overnight there. There's curb-cut access up to a cement walk over to the front door, but there aren't any accessible parking spaces on the restaurant side of the lot. That said, there are several accessible parking places in the Motel 6 lot, and there's even a larger parking space on the side of the restaurant (although it's not reserved for placard holders). Inside there's table seating with plenty of room for wheelchairs and scooters, and a barrier-free pathway to the accessible restrooms. Open all day, this popular restaurant serves up breakfast staples, soups, salads and sandwiches; and offers a nice selection of entrees and daily specials. There's also a soup and salad bar available, and several menu selections feature smaller portions for lighter eaters. On the other hand, some of the sandwiches and entrees are certainly large enough to share.

Bangkok Thai Cuisine

208 W. Andy Devine Avenue
Kingman, AZ 86401
(928) 753-1170

If you find yourself craving some Asian food in Kingman, then be sure and stop in at this hidden gem located next door to the Powerhouse Building. It's hard to miss as it's creatively decorated with colorful Route 66 murals. There's no accessible parking, however the parking lot is paved and level. There's also a barrier-free pathway to the restaurant from the accessible parking area next door. There's level access to the front door, with room for a wheelchair to maneuver around the tables. The menu includes a good selection of noodle, rice and curry dishes, and the quality is excellent. Top it off with good service and reasonable prices and you have a real winner. Don't let the lack of an accessible restroom deter you from enjoying this fine food, as accessible facilities are also available in the adjacent Powerhouse Building.

Bankok Thai Cuisine

Nearby

Hualapai Mountain Park

6250 Hualapai Mountain Road
Kingman, AZ 86401
(928) 681-5700
www.mcparks.com/parks/hualapai-mtn-park

Located on the outskirts of Kingman, this mountain park spans over 2,300 acres and offers some beautiful mountain views. If you'd like to overnight in the park, there's also a nice selection of accessible mountain cabins there. Additionally, there's a sizable elk population in the area, so there's no shortage of wildlife viewing opportunities. And even though Hualapai Mountain Park has a Kingman address, it's well away from the hustle and bustle of the city, which makes it the perfect place to spend a day or two on the way to or from the Grand Canyon.

Cabins

Cabin 9 (Timberline) is located in a small cabin loop, away from the busier areas of the park. It features accessible parking in a level cement driveway, with barrier-free access to the front door. Access features of the cabin include lever handles, wide doorways and a laminate floor. The great room includes a small kitchen nook with a refrigerator, a roll-under sink and a two-burner hot plate. There's a table with two benches in the adjacent area, along with a wood stove and a 27-inch high open-frame double bed. Although there's only 17 inches of clearance space between the table and the left side of the bed (as you face it), wheelchair access is possible if the table is moved.

The bathroom features a roll-in shower with grab bars and a slatted shower bench. The toilet is on a slight platform (presumably to accommodate the plumbing) and the seat is 21 inches high. It's located in a 36-inch wide alcove with grab bars on both sides and on the back wall. The only sink in this rustic cabin is the one in the kitchen area.

Outside there's a large level cement patio with an accessible picnic table, a fire circle and a grill. This cabin is also in a nice location as it overlooks other areas of the park. And although there are other cabins around, the pine forest provides a nice screen.

Visitors need to provide their own bedding, towels, kitchen utensils and dishes in this — and all — cabins in the park.

Cabin 24 is an accessible camping cabin, and it features parking in a level area with a sidewalk over to the front door. There's level access to the

Cabin 9 at Hualapai Mountain Park

Inside Cabin 9 at Hualapai Mountain Park (view 1)

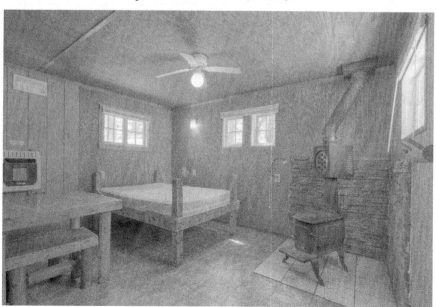

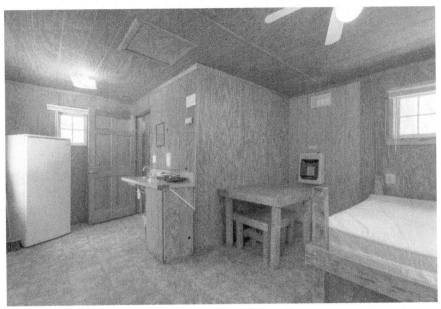

Inside Cabin 9 at Hualapai Mountain Park (view 2)

Bathroom in Cabin 9 at Hualapai Mountain Park

cabin, which is furnished with a double bunk bed, a table with benches, a microwave, a small refrigerator and a space heater. There's also a standard picnic table, grill and a fire circle on a level dirt area near the cabin.

This cabin does not have any water or bathroom facilities, but the accessible bathhouse is located across the street. The women's restroom includes an accessible stall with grab bars and a roll-under sink, while the men's restroom has a regular-sized stall with grab bars. A shower room, with a roll-in shower with grab bars and a shower bench, is located between the two restrooms.

Although there are no accessible trails in this hilly mountain park, the cabins provide a nice setting to enjoy the forest. You really don't have to go far for prime wildlife viewing either, and don't be surprised if the elk come right up to your cabin. As an added bonus, it's usually at least 10 degrees cooler in the park than in the city, so it's a great place to go to beat the heat in the summer.

Route 66 West

Route 66 — also known as Andy Devine Avenue — runs right through Kingman; and although there are a few vintage vestiges of the Mother Road along this six-mile urban stretch, it's definitely a modern-day experience. That said there are also two original sections of this historic road that begin on the east and west sides of town, which offer a glimpse at what Route 66 was like in its heyday.

The west section — also called the Oatman Highway — winds through the Black Mountains and over Sitgreaves Pass. Along the way this narrow road passes by the remnants of a bygone era, before it reconnects with Interstate 40, some 54 miles later. It takes about 1.5 hours to drive the route one-way, but it's best to allow extra time for plenty of stops, and lots of kitschy photos.

If you want to drive the entire route along the Mother Road, then bear left on Andy Devine Avenue at the Powerhouse Building and continue west on the two-lane road that parallels the freeway. Turn right at the stop sign at Shinarump Road, go under the interstate and make a left on Oatman Highway. Alternatively you can hop off Interstate 40 at exit 44 and follow the Route 66 signs.

Cool Springs

Cool Springs — which is barely more than a wide spot in the road — is located about 25 minutes west of Kingman. And although this rest stop was a welcome sight to weary Route 66 travelers, Hollywood also discovered it in 1992, when it was used as a filming location for Jean-Claude Van Damme's Universal Soldier. Sadly it was demolished in the final scenes of the movie; however it was later sold and rebuilt to resemble the original 1926 incarnation.

There's no striped parking at the site, but the dirt parking area is level. There's barrier-free access to the gift shop and museum through the main entrance, and even though there's one step inside, there's also level access to the raised area of the building from a second entrance. The makeshift museum offers up a quirky collection of found objects that includes everything from an old gas pump and tools, to oil cans, photos, toys and even vintage post cards. There's also a t-shirt shop, jewelry counter and a decent selection of Route 66 souvenirs peppered around the memorabilia.

Outside, there's an old 1935 rusted out Nash Sedan to the left of the store. And of course the old gas pump which rests under a restored stone canopy. Unfortunately there are no accessible restrooms at this stop, so plan ahead.

Cool Springs

Ruins of Ed's Camp on Oatman Highway

Sitgreaves Pass

From Cool Springs the Mother Road passes by the remnants of Ed's Camp and climbs up Gold Hill to Sitgreaves Pass. Hairpin turns and sheer drop-offs are the norm on this stretch of the road, and there's a noticeable lack of guard rails along the way. On the plus side, there's no shortage of spectacular windshield views, including a great one near the Mile-30 marker, and another one at the summit. After you reach the 3,550 foot summit, the downhill drive is just as exhilarating, with plenty of twists and turns along the way.

Oatman

Located just 20 minutes west of Cool Springs, Oatman was founded in 1906 to support the nearby gold mining camps. Today the town celebrates its rough and tumble past and retains a distinctive wild west flavor by holding daily gunfights in front of the Oatman Hotel. Scheduled for high noon and 2:15, these entertaining shootouts close down the road, so just sit back and enjoy, because you're not going anywhere until they're through.

There aren't any paved parking lots in town, and most people just park parallel along the main drag. There is however an accessible parking space located next to the post office on the east side of town. Some of the sidewalks are accessible, but many of the boardwalks have a few steps up to them. Most folks just walk or roll in the street as it's pretty safe because the motorists have to slow down to dodge the burros.

141

Burros in Oatman

Yes, I said burros. Years ago the miners used burros to work the gold mines, and today their descendants roam the streets of Oatman. A word of advice — guard your bags and purses, as they are very curious and they tend to chew on anything they can. Additionally watch where you walk or roll, because there are a lot of them. And if you'd like to feed them, there's no shortage of places that sell burro food.

All in all, Oatman is a fun stop, and although some of the shops have steps, there are also restaurants, stores and attractions that have level access. Additionally there are new accessible public restrooms on the east side of town.

Topock and Beyond

From Oatman it's a pleasant 35 minute drive to Topock, where you can connect to Interstate 40. This pleasant drive can be done as a loop, by taking Interstate 40 back to Kingman (it's about a one-hour drive); or as a one-way diversion on the way west to California.

Route 66 East

This slice of the Mother Road begins at the eastern end of Andy Devine Avenue, and continues along for 87 miles, before it ends in Seligman. It takes about 1.5 hours to drive it straight through, but as with the west section, allow plenty of extra time for stops along the way. On this section of the road you'll be treated to more than a few blasts from the past — including vintage Burma Shave billboards — as well as a number of roadside attractions, fun photo ops and historic sites.

Like the west section of the route, the east section can be accessed two ways. Again if you want to drive the entire length of Route 66, then just head east on Andy Devine Avenue from Kingman. After you pass the airport the road narrows to two lanes and meanders on towards Hackberry. Alternatively if you'd like to bypass the Kingman surface street traffic, then take Interstate 40 to exit 53 and head east towards the airport. On the plus side, unlike the west section of the road, this section of Route 66 is fairly level and straight.

Hackberry

About a half-hour down the road you'll come upon Hackberry; home of the Hackberry General Store, which features a vintage gas station, a souvenir shop and another great photo opportunity.

There's just a dirt parking area in front, but it is level and there's usually plenty of room to parallel park an adapted vehicle. Outside there's a treasure trove of memorabilia including some rusted out old cars, signs, tools and even a mock-up of a vintage garage. Additionally if you want to stop for a picnic lunch, there are several standard picnic tables on a level concrete pad in front of the store.

Hackberry General Store

There's level access to the store which offers souvenirs, cold drinks and snacks. And although the restrooms are not accessible, the men's room is worth a look as it's tastefully decorated with vintage pinup posters. Even if you can't go all the way in, take a gander at the interior from the doorway. Sadly the owner had to take down the posters of Farrah and Bo Derek, as they kept disappearing.

Valentine

The tiny hamlet of Valentine is just five miles up the road. Although there are a few remnants of an old hotel and gas station there, the big attraction is Keepers of the Wild. A scene from *Easy Rider* was also reportedly shot in this area.

Keepers of the Wild

13441 E. Highway 66
Valentine, Arizona 86437
(928) 769-1800
www.keepersofthewild.org

Located literally in the middle of nowhere, Keepers of the Wild houses over 150 exotic and indigenous animals that were rescued or abandoned. This non-profit animal sanctuary has a strict no breeding policy, with a strong focus on advocacy, education and protection. As part of their educational outreach, the facility is open to the public, and all admission fees go directly to the care of the animals.

Accessible parking is located in front of the gift shop, with a barrier-free pathway to the ticket counter inside. There are a few tables and chairs next to the accessible restrooms near the back of the gift shop, and there's level access out to the adjacent patio. The gift shop carries a wide variety of souvenir items including t-shirts, toys, puzzles, and even locally produced blown-out ostrich eggs. Hot dogs, burritos, nachos , breakfast sandwiches, snacks and drinks are also available. Additionally, there's a loaner wheelchair available — just ask for it at the front desk.

Outside there's level access from the patio to a dirt path over to the tour boarding area. Although visitors are welcome to walk around the sanctuary and check out all the habitats, the best way to learn about the animal residents is to also book a tram tour. It's important to remember to tell the folks at the ticket counter that you need the accessible tram tour, as some tours are conducted in inaccessible Pinzgauers — six-wheel drive decommissioned Swiss Army transport vehicles — which have three large steps in the rear.

Accessible tram at Keeoers of the Wild

There's room for two wheelchairs aboard the ramped open-air tram; which is also a good option for slow walkers who can only manage a small step. And if you can't manage the walk from the gift shop over to the boarding area, just let an employee know and they will be happy to take you over in a golf cart.

Although the tram tours are conducted several times each day, the prime tour time is at 3:30, as that's feeding time for the animals. The tour guides are great about pointing out natural animal behaviors and answering questions, but they also tell fascinating tales about how some of the current residents came to the facility. In short, most of the exotic animals were either illegally kept as pets and seized by wildlife officials, abandoned by their owners, or they are retired animal performers. On the other hand the indigenous species were usually abandoned by their mothers or illegally adopted by well meaning locals.

For example, there's the man who found a baby deer and took her to the local tavern to show his buddies. After wildlife officials seized her, she was placed at the sanctuary and appropriately named Brandy. And then there's Sabrina the liger — a cross between a male lion and a female tiger — that was bred as a novelty. A group of wolves came to Keepers of the Wild after their owner had to leave them behind when he evacuated the Butte Fire in Northern California. He expected to find them dead when he returned —

after all his car was melted — but instead they survived by burrowing down 15 feet to create a safe den. Unfortunately the fire evacuee had problems relocating with the wolves, so he sought out a good home for his beloved pack. And let's not even talk about the 148 monkeys found inside a home of an animal hoarder in Maricopa, which were relocated to the sanctuary by the local sheriff. You'll hear all these stories and more on the excellent tram tour.

Save some time to explore the sanctuary on your own too. Some of the lower dirt pathways are accessible in good weather — remember it can snow there in the winter — and the steeper ones are covered on the tram tour. It's a great attraction, and the staff is very well versed in access issues. Keepers of the Wild is really a must-see on this stretch of Route 66.

Peach Springs
Peach Springs, which is about 20 minutes east of Valentine, is probably the most sizable burg along this section of Route 66. Located on Hualapai land, it boasts a hotel, a restaurant, a gas station, a cultural center, and a few vintage buildings. It's also the gateway to a little-known driving route down to the Colorado River, at the bottom of the Grand Canyon.

Hualapai Cultural Center
Built on the site of the Qumacho Cafe, the Hualapai Cultural Center is one of the newer additions to the community. Open Monday through Friday, the center serves to preserve and promote Hualapai culture, through public education and cultural programs. Accessible parking is available on a concrete slab to the far left of the building, with level access to the front door. Inside, there is barrier-free access to all areas with plenty of room to navigate a wheelchair. Although there's no formal tour, the receptionist is happy to show visitors around and answer questions. The cultural center features a nice collection of native artwork, as well as baskets, pottery and other items created by the young people of the tribe.

Osterman Gas Station
Remnants of the past can also be seen in Peach Springs at the Osterman Shell Station. There's level access over to this deserted building, which is located between the Hualapai Cultural Center and Hualapai Lodge. This former Shell station, which was built by Oscar Osterman in the 1920s, did a robust business during the boom days of Route 66. Sadly when the Mother Road was decommissioned, business died off and eventually the business was closed. The building was placed on the National Register in 2012.

Hualapai Cultural Center

Diamond Creek Road

Peach Springs is also the gateway to the 19.5-mile Diamond Creek Road driving route to the bottom of the Grand Canyon. It's an excellent choice for wheelchair-users and slow walkers, as there's no shortage of great windshield views along the way. A permit, which is required to drive the bottom of the canyon, can be purchased at the Hualapai Fish and Game Office, which is located across the street from the Hualapai Cultural Center. There are several steps up to this historic building, which once operated as a trading post.

Diamond Creek Road is located across the street from Hualapai Lodge. The drive begins as a paved road, but the pavement quickly gives way to a graded dirt road. A four-wheel drive vehicle is recommend for the drive, as the road gets rockier as it nears the river. There are a couple of shaded picnic tables on the beach, which can usually be reached in dry weather. Even if you don't make it all the way to the river, it's still a beautiful drive.

Walapai Market & Gas

Located across the street from the historic Osterman Gas Station, this new market and gas station offers a variety of traveler services. Accessible parking is located behind the building, with level access to both the market and the gas station. The market features level access and includes a deli, a bakery and a wide selection of grocery items. Made-to-order sandwiches and pizza are also available. Outside there's level access to a comfortable seating area with tables and chairs, and barrier-free access to the adjacent gas station. It's a good place to take a break, get some gas and grab a cold drink.

Hualapai Lodge

900 AZ-66
Peach Springs, AZ 86434
(928) 769-2230
www.grandcanyonwest.com

Located on the south side of Route 66, Hualapai Lodge retains the flavor of yesteryear, but offers a long list of modern day amenities. There's accessible parking in front, with level access to the building, and a barrier-free pathway to the front desk. The lobby boasts a cozy river rock fireplace, and the walls are tastefully adorned with Hualapai artwork.

Accessible room 115 is located just off the lobby. This extra-large room features wide doorways, a lowered peephole and good pathway access. It's furnished with two 26-inch high open-frame queen-sized beds, with wheelchair access in the middle. Other furnishings include an easy chair, a chest of drawers and a desk with a chair. There's also a refrigerator and a microwave in the room.

The bathroom features a wide doorway and is equipped with a roll-in

Hualapai Lodge

Bedroom in room 115 in Hualapai Lodge

shower with a hand-held showerhead and a fold-down shower bench. Toilet grab bars are located on the back and left walls (as seated), and a roll-under sink is located in an alcove just outside the bathroom.

Room 116, which is located across the hall, includes the same access features and bed configuration, except that the toilet grab bars are located on the back and right walls (as seated).

There's barrier-free access to all the public areas of the property, including

Bathroom in room 115 at Hualapai Lodge

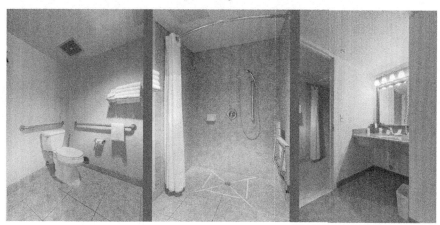

the pool and spa area which is equipped with a portable lift. The Diamond Creek Restaurant, which is just down the hall from the lobby, features level access and offers a menu filled with Native American specialties and traditional American favorites. Accessible restrooms are located near the restaurant.

Hualapai Lodge is a good choice for folks who want to explore Route 66 or drive down to the Colorado River at the bottom of the Grand Canyon. It's a clean, comfortable and affordable property.

Grand Canyon Caverns

Located about 10 minutes down the road from Peach Springs, Grand Canyon Caverns is also worth a stop. A large sign marks the entrance to the mile-long flag-lined road that leads to this family-owned attraction. Take a few minutes to have a look at the vintage automobiles near the beginning of the road too, at aptly named Radiator Springs.

Although there's no accessible parking at Grand Canyon Caverns, the large lot is paved, and there's usually plenty of room to parallel park an adapted van. And don't forget to snap a photo of the large dinosaur that guards the entrance to this vintage attraction. From the parking area, there's level access over to the ramped entry to the restaurant, and barrier-free access to the ticket counter next door. Accessible restrooms are also located near the restaurant.

Grand Canyon Caverns

Although none of the cavern tours are technically wheelchair-accessible, the Short Tour may work for some wheelchair-users and slow walkers. This half-hour tour travels about a quarter-mile on paved trails, although manual wheelchair-users may need some assistance with some of the grades. There's elevator access down to the entrance, and although there are 15 steps at the beginning of the tour, there's also an alternate step-free route for folks who cannot manage them. Additionally, a loaner wheelchair and walker are available.

The Short Tour passes through the Chapel of the Ages, and around the Caverns Suite (an actual underground hotel room), and continues past the Grotto Restaurant before it returns to the entrance. Along the way visitors are treated to a good sampling of rock formations as they learn about the history of the attraction, which was once only accessible by a rope. It's a fun tour, and although the pathways through the caverns were constructed before there were any access laws on the books, the owners have done their best to make this tour as accessible as possible.

Seligman

Known as the birthplace of the "preserve Route 66 movement", Seligman is located about a half-hour from Grand Canyon Caverns at the end of the east section of Route 66. It's the home town of Angel Delgadillo, the founder

Snow Cap Drive-In in Seligman

of the Historic Route 66 Association, and the man who spearheaded efforts to restore part of the Mother Road.

Street parking is the norm in this little burg; but the good news is that sidewalks and curb-cuts have been added for better access. Many of the historic buildings have been converted to gift shops, and although a few have a step or two at the entrance, a good number of them also offer level access. It's fun to just stroll down the street and look at the different storefronts.

Make sure and stop in at the Snow Cap Drive-In, which was built from scrap lumber by Juan Delgadillo in 1953. There's level access from the street to the counter — where you can place your order — and plenty of room for a wheelchair or scooter on the large patio dining area. There's also a nice collection of vintage cars behind the restaurant in a level area, as well as more tables for overflow dining.

From Seligman, you can either hop on Interstate 40 and head back to Kingman (an hour drive), or continue east for another 1.5 hours to the South Rim of the Grand Canyon.

Chloride

Known as the oldest continually inhabited mining town in Arizona, Chloride is located about 25 miles north of Kingman, off of Highway 93. It makes a good side trip from Kingman, or a fun stop along the way to Grand

Yesterdays Restaurant in Chloride

Canyon West. From Highway 93, head east on Road 125 for about four miles until you cross a cattle guard and enter Chloride.

There's not much in the way of services in this tiny town, which has a population of about 300 people; but there is a small market, a visitor center, a post office and a restaurant and bar. There's one accessible parking space near the Mineshaft Market on Tennessee Street, with ramp access up to the front porch and level access through the front door. Yesterdays Restaurant, which is located on 2nd Street, also has accessible parking in front with level access to the restaurant. And even the Prospector Cafe and Bar on Tennessee Street has a cement ramp in the front.

Chloride is known for its yard art made from found objects, so take some time to stroll around the town to admire the installations. The main roads are pretty level, and it's an excellent photo op. And if you visit on a Saturday, there's usually a gunfight downtown at high noon.

Chloride is also known for Roy Purcell's murals that are painted on some rocky outcroppings in the hills outside town. Just follow Tennessee Street across the far cattle guard and continue along the dirt road to the mural site. Although a four-wheel-drive vehicle is not required, this road isn't passable in a low-clearance vehicle either. The 1.4-mile drive is quite manageable in most SUVs and trucks, and once you arrive at the site, there's a large level area to pull over and park.

Roy Purcell's murals Just outside Chloride

Painted in the mid-60s, the murals have weathered the test of time quite well, as the vibrant colors still really pop. Titled "The Journey" the murals include images of a snake that winds through several frames and ultimately eats the sun, a talon that looms over Chloride, fertility images, pieces with a definite Yin and Yang side, astrological signs and many scenes that are open to interpretation. Stay a while to study the drawings, as the longer you look at them, the more hidden details you'll spot.

Williams

Elevation 6,766 feet

B illed as the gateway to the Grand Canyon, Williams is located about an hour south of the South Rim. This friendly town, which is filled with Route 66 history, and fun if not kitschy attractions, makes a convenient home base for any Grand Canyon road trip. Alternatively, you can take the train from Williams to the South Rim and spend the day in the popular national park, or linger on for a few days in one of the South Rim hotels. Either way, Williams is definitely worth a spot on any Grand Canyon itinerary.

Attractions

Williams Visitor Center

200 W. Railroad Avenue
Williams, AZ 86046
(928) 635-4061
www.experiencewilliams.com

There's accessible parking in the large lot behind the visitor center, with barrier-free access to the entrance. Inside there's plenty of room to maneuver a wheelchair around the exhibits and brochures, and barrier-free access over to the staffed information desk. Some Grand Canyon excursions can also be booked there. Accessible restrooms are located in the back of the building. This is a good first stop for Williams visitors, as this information center is well stocked with maps and brochures on local attractions.

Williams Historic Walking Tour

Pick up a free Historic Walking Tour Map at the visitor center and explore the downtown area on foot. From the visitor center, head west on Railroad Avenue, turn south on Fourth Street, then make a left on Route 66. From there continue along this historic stretch of road, past the former saloons, gas stations, pool halls and grocery stores to First Street, then head north to Railroad Avenue to complete the loop.

Be sure and stop in at Pete's Gas Station & Museum at First and Route 66 along the way. There's level access to a small display in the mechanic's bay, which includes old tools, car parts, manuals, signs and even a vintage phone and cash register.

The walking tour route is fairly level, although some of the brick sidewalks and worn curb-cuts are a bit bumpy. It's only a three-block walk, and there are lots of shops and galleries — many of which have level access — to stop in along the way. As an added bonus, you can do as little or as much of the tour as you want.

Bearizona

1500 E. Route 66
Williams, AZ 86046
(928) 635-2289
www.bearizona.com

This drive-through wildlife park features a robust collection of North American wildlife, and offers visitors an up-close-and-personal look at the residents. The 160-acre park is home to a large number of rescued and rehabilitated animals, and also includes animals that are on loan for propagation.

Visitors can drive their own vehicles through the three-mile wildlife drive, and spot Rocky Mountain goats, American bison, Alaskan tundra wolves, Dall sheep and black bears along the way. Best of all, you can drive through the compound as many times as you want during the day, which allows for a wide range of animal sightings. And since you drive your own vehicle, it's nicely accessible.

At the end of the wildlife drive, you'll find Fort Bearizona, which is home to a collection of small or juvenile animals. There's accessible parking near the entrance, with wide level paved pathways past all of the animal enclosures in the

Pete's Gas Station and Museum in Williams

20-acre walk-through area. You'll see everything from javelinas and lynxes to porcupines, beavers, swift foxes and of course, lots of juvenile black bears. Loaner wheelchairs are available near the entrance, and there's also barrier-free access to the public areas — including the gift shops and restrooms — at Fort Bearizona.

Make sure and time your visit so you can take in the raptor show, which is presented daily from March through December, and on weekends in January and February. This free-flight show features high country raptors including hawks, owls and eagles. Wheelchair seating for the show is available in a cement area, with companion seats located nearby.

The best plan of action is to visit Bearizona in the morning, as the animals are more active then. And don't forget, Bearizona is a work in progress, so come back often to check out the new programs and facilities. You'll never see the same thing twice at Bearizona, and that's a very good thing.

Deer Farm

6769 E. Deer Farm Road
Williams, AZ 86046
(928) 635-4073
www.deerfarm.com

Located east of town, just off historic Route 66, the Deer Farm make a good stop if you have kids in tow. There's no striped parking but the lot is paved

Black bears frolicking at Bearizona

and level, and there's ramp access up to the large gift shop, where admission tickets are sold. Accessible restrooms are also located in the gift shop.

Paved pathways lead through the park, where deer roam free and visitors are encouraged to feed them. There are also a number of enclosures that house everything from bison, alpacas and reindeer, to porcupines, pygmy goats and even a marmoset. And don't miss Gracie the camel, who will give you a kiss if you offer her a carrot.

Grand Canyon Railway

233 N. Grand Canyon Boulevard
Williams, AZ 86046
(800) 843-8724
www.thetrain.com

If you'd like to leave the driving to someone else, then head up to the South Rim on the Grand Canyon Railway. This historic excursion runs along Highway 64, and travels from Williams to Grand Canyon Village. Although the railway dates back to 1901, access upgrades have been added over the years, so today it's a suitable option for wheelchair-users and slow walkers. And with a variety of packages available, you can opt to spend the afternoon in the park, or extend your stay and overnight in one of the accessible South Rim properties.

Gracie, the kissing camel

The Depot

The Grand Canyon Railway departs from the historic Williams Depot, located right behind the Grand Canyon Railway Hotel. There is level access to the train depot, gift shop and coffee stand, and an accessible restroom is located in the back.

The Fray Marcos Hotel — which opened to the public in 1908 — once occupied the left portion of the depot. Today most vestiges of this 43-room Harvey House are gone, however there are some vintage photos in the former lobby which is located next to the gift shop.

Prior to the Grand Canyon Railway departure from the Williams Depot, there is a wild west shootout, which features the local marshal and the nefarious Cataract Creek Gang. There is level access to the show area, which is located next to the depot. Wheelchair-accessible seating is available for the show, in front of the bleachers or at nearby tables.

Access Aboard

After the wild west shootout, a preboarding announcement is made, and wheelchair-users and slow walkers are boarded before the rest of the passengers. Access is good on this historic train; and train buffs are wowed by the vintage train cars which are pulled by diesel locomotives. There are six classes of service, with Pullman, Coach and First Class being the most accessible.

Cataract Creek Gang stage a wild west shootout

The Harriman-Style Pullman cars have bench seats that flip so families can sit together, while the Budd coach cars have front facing bench seats and air conditioning. The first-class cars have comfortable reclining seats, large windows and air conditioning. All of these cars can be accessed by a portable lift, and they all have wheelchair tie-downs, nearby companion seats and an accessible restroom with grab bars, a wide doorway and ample room to transfer. Power outlets are located near the accessible seats, and the lifts are large enough to accommodate scooters and heavy power wheelchairs.

The Luxury Parlor Car can also be accessed by the lift, but it has table-and-chair seating and no tie-downs, so a transfer is necessary. This class of service is really best suited for slow walkers.

Grand Canyon Railway also offers two classes of service in multi-level domed cars — the Observation Dome and the Luxury Dome. Because of the configuration of these cars, and the fact that they have stairs to the upper levels, these classes of service are not a good choice for most wheelchair-users. Passengers need to be able to walk the length of a railcar and climb up and down a staircase in order to use these classes of service.

And of course, if you just can't make up your mind about which class to book, you can always mix classes; and take one class going up and another on the return trip.

Boarding the Grand Canyon Railway

The Route

The train travels due north to the Grand Canyon's South Rim, and passes through a Ponderosa Pine forest outside Williams, before it drops down to an open prairie, and then climbs back up to the Pinyon Pine forest near the Grand Canyon.

Passengers in First Class and the Luxury Parlor Car are offered complimentary snacks and bar service during the journey; while soft drinks are served in Coach and Pullman Class.

During the two-hour journey, roving musicians entertain passengers with western songs, while on-board attendants are available to field questions about activities at the South Rim. And on the return trip, keep a lookout for a return appearance of the Cataract Creek Gang.

The train makes two daily round-trips to the South Rim in the summer; and one a day the rest of the year. Most people go up and back on the same day, but you can also purchase a package that includes overnight accommodations in an accessible room at Maswik Lodge. Alternatively, you can extend your South Rim stay for several days if you like, as trains run up and back every day.

Best of all, the Grand Canyon Railway employees are very accommodating, so make sure and let them know if you have any access needs; especially if your disability isn't readily apparent. They are also happy to answer questions and even provide suggestions to help make your trip more comfortable.

Lodging

Grand Canyon Railway Hotel

233 N. Grand Canyon Boulevard
Williams, AZ 86046
(800) 843-8724
www.thetrain.com

Located next to the Grand Canyon Railway Depot and just a block from historic Route 66, this 297-room property offers accessible rooms that are equipped with either a roll-in shower or a tub/shower combination. Accessible parking is located near the front entrance, with level access to the lobby. There's also a level drop-off area by the front door.

Room 1116 is a standard accessible room. Access features include wide doorways, a lowered peephole, lever handles and a lowered closet rod. It's furnished with two 25-inch high queen-sized beds with wheelchair access between them, a desk with a chair, an easy chair and a refrigerator.

The bathroom includes a roll-in shower with grab bars, a hand-held showerhead and a portable shower bench. The toilet grab bars are located on the back and left walls (as seated). Other access features include a roll-under sink, a lowered hair dryer and a lowered clothing hook.

Bedroom in room 1116 at the Grand Canyon Railway Hotel

Bathroom in room 1116 at the Grand Canyon Railway Hotel

Room 1314 includes the same basic access features and furnishings, but it is a mirror image of room 1116, so the toilet grab bars are located on the back and right walls (as seated). It also has a fold-down shower bench in addition to the portable shower bench.

Bathroom in room 1314 at the Grand Canyon Railway Hotel

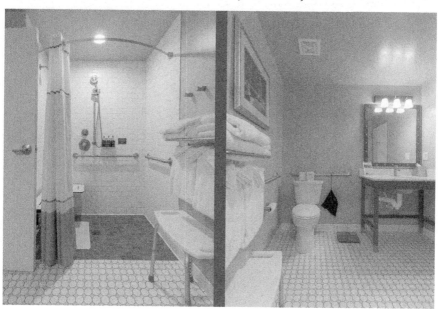

Room 1306 is a deluxe accessible room. It includes the same basic access features and furnishings as room 1116, except that the beds are 27-inches high. The bathroom is equipped with a roll-in shower with a hand-held showerhead, grab bars and a fold-down shower bench. The toilet grab bars are located on the back and right walls (as seated), and the bathroom has a roll-under sink. There's also a portable shower bench in the bathroom.

Room 1308 is also a deluxe accessible room, It includes the same basic access features as room 1306, except that it has a tub/shower combination with grab bars, a hand-held showerhead and a portable shower bench. The toilet grab bars are located on the back and left walls (as seated), and the bathroom also has a roll-under sink.

Room 1326 is an accessible suite. Access features include wide doorways, a lowered peephole and good pathway access. It includes a kitchenette that's equipped with a refrigerator, a microwave and a wet bar; and an adjacent sitting area that's furnished with a 14-inch high sleeper sofa. The spacious bedroom features two 27-inch high queen-sized beds, with wheelchair access between them, a desk with a chair, night tables, an easy chair and an armoire.

The bathroom is equipped with a roll-in shower with a hand-held showerhead, grab bars and a portable shower chair. Other access features include toilet grab bars on the back and right walls (as seated), and a roll-under sink.

Bathroom in room 1308 at the Grand Canyon Railway Hotel

The property also has an accessible suite with two queen-sized beds and an accessible tub/shower combination.

Additionally, toilet risers and portable shower chairs are available for any room, on request.

Access is good to all the public areas at the Grand Canyon Railway Hotel, including the fitness center, business center, and the lift-equipped pool and spa. There's elevator access to all levels, which gives wheelchair-users and slow walkers access to the upstairs game room and the sitting area that overlooks the main lobby

There is also level access to Spenser's Pub, which is located near the lobby in the main hotel building. This casual eatery offers a light bar menu and a large selection of libations. Patio dining is also available during the warmer months.

Customer service is top-drawer at the Grand Canyon Railway Hotel too, so don't be afraid to ask if you need anything. It's a very comfortable, accessible and friendly place to stay.

Best Western Plus Inn of Williams

2600 W. Route 66
Williams, AZ 86046
(928) 635-4400
www.bestwestern.com

Although this three-diamond property is located on historic Route 66, it's nestled away on a secluded mountainside in a pleasant pine and oak forest. There's accessible parking near the entrance, with level access to the lobby, which is decorated with Kachina dolls and Native American artifacts.

Room 110 is located on the first floor, just a short walk from the lobby. Access features include wide doorways, a lowered peephole, low-pile carpet and laminate flooring, and good pathway access.

It's furnished with a 28-inch high king-sized bed with wheelchair access on both sides, a night table, a chest of drawers, a desk with a chair, an easy chair with an ottoman, and a refrigerator. There's also a roll-under sink outside of the bathroom.

The bathroom is equipped with a roll-in shower with grab bars, a hand-held showerhead and a portable shower bench. There are also toilet grab bars on the back, right and front walls (as seated).

Room 102, which is located down the hall, has the same access features,

Bedroom in room 110 at the Best western Plus Inn of Williams

furnishings and bed configuration as room 110, except that it also has a lowered clothing rod.

Room 104 has the same basic access features and furnishings as Room 102, but since it's a mirror image of that room, the toilet grab bars are located on the back, left and front walls (as seated).

There's level access to the public areas of the property, including the dining room, lounge, fitness center and business center. There is also elevator access to the upper floors. The pool is located just outside the back door,

Bathroom in room 110 at the Best western Plus Inn of Williams

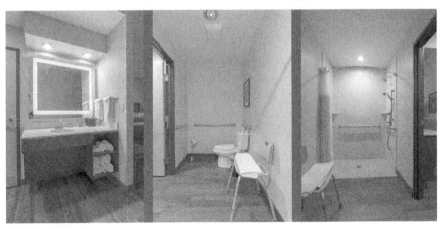

Bathroom in room 104 at the Best western Plus Inn of Williams

and it features ramp access, barrier-free pathways around the deck, and a pool lift. The spa is located in a separate enclosure that's shaded by the surrounding oaks. It features level access and a spa lift.

It's a very comfortable property in a relaxing setting, and the employees go out of their way to make guests feel at home.

Dining

Grand Depot Café

233 N. Grand Canyon Boulevard
Williams, AZ 86046
(928) 635-4010
www.thetrain.com

Located next to the Williams Railroad Depot, the Grand Depot Café features ramp access, with plenty of room to maneuver a wheelchair inside. This buffet-style restaurant serves breakfast, lunch and dinner, and features a fresh selection of traditional fare, as well Harvey House specialties from the past, such as Harvey Girl Orange Pancakes and Chicken Maciel. A carving station and a pasta bar are also available in the evening. And if you need help carrying your tray, staff members are happy to assist.

Cruiser's Cafe 66

233 W. Route 66
Williams, AZ 86046
(928) 635-2445
www.cruisers66.com

Located on Route 66 in downtown Williams, Cruiser's Cafe 66 was a gas station back in the Mother Road's heyday. Today the vintage gas pump still graces the front, while the walls of the eatery are covered with kitschy memorabilia. There's level access to the outdoor dining area, which offers a prime view of Route 66. There's table seating on the patio, but only booth seating inside. An accessible restroom is located near the bar; however there's one step up to the entrance. The menu offers a good selection of burgers, sandwiches and BBQ plates; and although the offerings are largely beef and pork, there are a few chicken items included. It's also a fun place to stop in for a beer.

Red Raven Restaurant

135 W. Route 66
Williams, AZ 86046
(928) 635-4980
www.redravenrestaurant.com

There's no accessible parking in front of this downtown eatery, but accessible parking is available in the visitor center lot, which is just a short level block away. There's ramp access up to this historic building, but it's fairly steep and most folks will need some assistance. Inside, there's plenty of room to maneuver a wheelchair around the tables, and single-use accessible restrooms are located in the rear of the building. Open for lunch and dinner, this casual fine dining restaurant serves up a creative selection of fresh entrees, sandwiches, wraps and healthy salads. It's a local favorite, and as a added bonus they also have a substantial wine list.

Nearby

Arizona Raft Adventures

(800) 786-7238
www.azraft.com

If you'd like to take a rafting trip through the Grand Canyon on the Colorado River, then contact the folks at Arizona Rafting Adventures. They are experts at making things work for manual wheelchair-users and slow walkers; and they have worked with Wounded Warriors and No Barriers to provide multi-day rafting trips to amputees and people with Cerebral Palsy and Multiple Sclerosis. Unfortunately there is no way to recharge wheelchair batteries on these remote camping trips. so they are not really a good option for power wheelchair-users.

The 8-10 day accessible trips are conducted in motorized rafts, which have plenty of room to carry the extra adaptive equipment. Although a variety of accessible raft seating options are available, the torso stabilizing chair is the most popular one. Adaptive camping equipment includes portable tracking (mats) to lay over the sand at the campsites, a toilet tent, a porta-potty railing and a wheelchair chariot which allows staff to carry non-ambulatory guests. Additionally, they also have an inflatable kayak so guests can enjoy the side canyon hikes with water.

The folks at Arizona Rafting Adventures realize that everybody is different, and they work closely with their disabled guests to provide them with the most accessible rafting experience possible.

Flagstaff

Elevation 6,910 feet

Located just 90 minutes from the South Rim, Flagstaff makes a good home base for Grand Canyon visitors. And the scenic drive down Highway 180 is a must-do, even if you overnight elsewhere. Flagstaff is also the location of the closest commercial airport to the South Rim, so it's a good fly-drive choice; and since the city boasts a number of popular attractions, it's an equally interesting post trip for west-bound Grand Canyon visitors. Last but certainly not least, Flagstaff also serves as the gateway to a number of nearby natural areas and attractions.

Attractions

Flagstaff Visitor Center

1 E. Route East 66
Flagstaff, AZ 86001
(928) 213-2951
www.flagstaffarizona.org

There's accessible parking in the small lot next to the Flagstaff Visitor Center, which is located in a 1926 rail depot building, which today also serves as an

Flagstaff Visitor Center

Amtrak station. There's level access to the building, which offers a staffed information desk, a nice collection of brochures and maps, and a gift shop. Accessible restrooms are located between the information desk and the Amtrak station. It's a good Flagstaff first stop, however rail buffs may want to hang out a bit longer to see — and photograph — the passing trains.

Flagstaff Route 66 Walking Tour

Pick up a walking tour map and brochure at the Flagstaff Visitor Center, and set out to see some remnants of the Mother Road in the downtown area. The tour starts at the visitor center, which is located on Route 66; and although the whole tour is not wheelchair-accessible, there's a nice half-mile loop that includes some vintage sites.

From the visitor center head east down the sidewalk in front of the building to San Francisco Street. You can cross the street to see the 1897 depot and the old steam engine parked at Santa Fe Plaza at this intersection; but you'll need to return to the west side of the street for the accessible path across the railroad tracks. Continue down to Phoenix Street and cross the street, and walk past the former Downtown Motel (now the Grand Canyon International Hostel) and the Motel DeBeau (now the Travelers Inn). Note that the original signs still stand at these once popular Route 66 properties. And don't miss the Route 66 mural on the brick building across the street. Continue along Phoenix Street until you hit Beaver Street. The official route continues along Phoenix, but the

Original sign at the Motel DeBeau

Mural on the Flagstaff Route 66 Walking Tour

sidewalks are not accessible, so cross Beaver Street, turn right and head back to the depot. And of course, don't forget to get your photo taken by the Route 66 emblem in the visitor center parking lot. It's a fun little jaunt, and the brochure details the history of the downtown buildings.

Museum of Northern Arizona

3101 N. Fort Valley Road
Flagstaff, AZ 86001
(928) 774-5213
www.musnaz.org

There's accessible parking and ramp access up to this excellent museum, which is housed in a historic 1936 malpais (lava rock) building. There's good access throughout the galleries which contain exhibits about the archeology, paleontology, geology and native peoples of the Colorado Plateau. The recently opened Gallery of Native Peoples of the Colorado Plateau includes exhibits on the Hopi, Ute, Paiute, Havasupai, Hualapai, Yavapai-Apache, Navajo, Acoma and Zuni peoples. The displays help lend insight into the customs, traditions and values of these Native Americans, and serve to point out their commonalities and differences. There's also an excellent gallery which includes pottery and jewelry of the native peoples, as well as several rooms that feature changing exhibitions. There's something tucked away in just about every nook and cranny of this Depression-era

Museum of Northern Arizona

building. The museum shop also offers a good selection of jewelry, and since it's operated by a non-profit, there's no sales tax.

Riordin Mansion

409 W. Riordan Road
Flagstaff, AZ 86001
(928) 779-4395
www.azstateparks.com/riordan-mansion

This 13,000-square foot mansion was built by Irish immigrants Timothy and Michael Riordan, who developed a successful Flagstaff logging business in the early 1900s. Interestingly enough, the brothers married sisters, and each couple lived in one wing of this 40-room Craftsman-style house. And if you see a resemblance to El Tovar on Grand Canyon's South Rim, that's because the same architect — Charles Whittlesey — designed both structures.

There's accessible parking near the mansion, with level access to the visitor center. Inside there's plenty of room to maneuver a wheelchair around the interpretive exhibits, and barrier-free access to the accessible restrooms. The only way to see the inside of the mansion is on a guided tour, which is partially accessible.

There's alternative ramp access up to the east wing entrance, and from there wheelchair-users can access all the downstairs rooms on the tour, including the back porch, living room, kitchen, dining room, serving pantry, library and reception hall. The upstairs part of the tour, which includes the bedrooms, is not accessible; however a movie of this area is available at the visitor center. The tour ends on the first-floor east wing, which includes interpretive exhibits and more information about the family. It's an excellent tour, and 95% of the furnishings in the home are original.

There's also a self-guided walking tour that leads around the outside of the house, and features a good interpretation of the home and the family. There's no cost to walk around the grounds, but there is a 50 cent charge for an informative brochure and map. Although the asphalt walkway along the route is level, there are a few cracks here and there. Even if you don't take the home tour, plan for a leisurely stroll around the grounds. Additionally there's an accessible picnic table located near the parking lot.

Lowell Observatory

1400 W. Mars Hill Road
Flagstaff, AZ 86001
(928) 774-3358
www.lowell.edu

Located on a prominent hill in town, the Lowell Observatory was developed by Percival Lowell to search for evidence of life on Mars. Interestingly enough, a young Clyde Tombaugh discovered Pluto there some 26 years later. Unfortunately most of the campus is pretty hilly, so the walking tours that highlight the different telescopes are not accessible. That said, this site is definitely worth a stop if you time your visit right.

There's accessible parking in front of the visitor center, with ramp access up to the front door. Inside there's barrier-free access to the information desk, gift shop and accessible restrooms. There's also an accessible picnic area located out back in a shaded grove.

There's ramp access up to the Rotunda Museum, which is a short level walk from the visitor center; however the side ramp leads up to the business office, so let the front desk person know if you cannot manage the stairs at the museum entrance. The small museum has a number of interesting displays, and includes an informative panel on how Pluto was named (hint — it had nothing to do with Walt Disney). Evening programs are also presented in this building.

In order to make the best use of your time, consult the observatory website for a schedule of their daily programs. Best bet is to pack along a picnic dinner, and hit the observatory around 4:00 p.m. Check out the Rotunda Museum first, then wander back to the visitor center for some solar viewing from the portable telescope on the back patio. At 5:00 p.m., there's usually an evening program in the Rotunda Museum, after which you can enjoy dinner al fresco in the picnic area. Some days there is also a science talk at 7:00 p.m. in the visitor center. Top off your visit with a little star gazing through the portable telescopes on the back patio. It takes a little planning, but it is possible to enjoy an accessible and informative visit — just remember to check the schedule on the website.

Lodging

Hampton Inn & Suites Flagstaff East

990 N. Country Club Drive
Flagstaff, AZ 86004
(928) 433-1234
www.hamptoninn.com

Located off Interstate 40 at Country Club Drive, the Hampton Inn & Suites Flagstaff East is one of the city's newer properties. Opened in late 2017 it exudes a hip cool vibe, with light colors, clean lines and sleek furnishings. Accessible parking is available near the front entrance, with level access over to the lobby through automatic doors. This property has accessible rooms that are equipped with either a roll-in shower or a tub/shower combination.

Room 130, which is located on the ground floor, features wide doorways, lever handles, excellent pathway access and a lowered closet rod. It's furnished with a 26-inch high king-sized bed with wheelchair access on both sides, a compact chest of drawers, a desk with a chair, and a 15-inch high sleeper sofa. There's also a wet bar with a microwave and a refrigerator in the cavernous room.

The bathroom features a sliding door and includes a full five-foot turning radius. It's equipped with a roll-in shower with grab bars, a hand-held showerhead and a fold-down shower bench. The toilet grab bars are located on the back and left walls (as seated), and the bathroom also includes a roll-under sink. Even the little things — like a lowered robe hook — were figured into the access plan of this well equipped room.

Room 224, which is located on the second floor, features wide doorways, a lowered peephole, lever handles, and good pathway access. It's furnished with a king-sized bed with wheelchair access on both sides, a desk with a chair, and

Bedroom in room 130 at Hampton Inn & Suites Flagstaff East (view 1)

Bedroom in room 130 at Hampton Inn & Suites Flagstaff East (view 2)

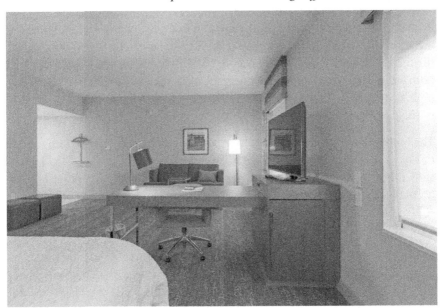

Bathroom in room 130 at Hampton Inn & Suites Flagstaff East (view 2)

an easy chair. It also includes a refrigerator and a microwave.

The bathroom features a sliding door and includes a full five-foot turning radius. It's furnished with a tub/shower combination with grab bars, a hand-held showerhead and a movable slatted shower bench. The toilet grab bars are located on the back and left walls (as seated), and the bathroom also has a roll-under sink.

There's elevator access to all floors of this property, and barrier-free access to all the public areas, including the first-floor guest laundry, fitness room

Bedroom in room 224 at Hampton Inn & Suites Flagstaff East

Bathroom in room 224 at Hampton Inn & Suites Flagstaff East

and breakfast room. Accessible restrooms are also located just off the lobby. There's level access to the lift-equipped indoor pool and spa, which is located on the first floor near the elevator; and level access to the adjacent patio. There's also an accessible family restroom in the pool area.

It's a fun property, with excellent access and a very accommodating staff.

Fairfield Inn & Suites Flagstaff East

1000 N. Country Club Drive
Flagstaff, AZ 86004
(928) 707-7800
www.fairfield.marriott.com

Located next door to the Hampton Inn, the Fairfield Inn & Suites Flagstaff East was also constructed in 2017. Accessible parking is located near the entrance, with a barrier-free pathway through the automatic lobby doors. Inside there's barrier-free access throughout the inviting lobby, and over to the registration desk. In contrast to the Hampton Inn, this property is decorated in a warm palette and uses darker wood with splashes of vibrant accent colors in a decidedly retro theme. It features accessible rooms that are equipped with either a roll-in shower or a tub/shower combination.

Room 225, which is a standard queen, features wide doorways, a lowered peephole, low-pile carpet, lever handles and a lowered closet rod. It's furnished with two 29-inch high queen-sized beds with wheelchair access between them, a desk with a chair, and a chest of drawers. It also includes a microwave and a refrigerator.

The bathroom is equipped with a tub/shower combination with grab bars

Bedroom in room 225 at Fairfield Inn & Suites

and a hand-held showerhead. The toilet grab bars are located on the back and left walls (as seated), and the bathroom also has a roll-under sink. A portable shower bench is available upon request.

Room 203 is a standard king with the same basic access features as room 225. It's furnished with a 29-inch high king-sized bed with wheelchair access on both sides, a desk with a chair, a chest of drawers, a refrigerator and a microwave.

The bathroom is equipped with a 36-inch-square transfer-type shower with

Bathroom in room 225 at Fairfield Inn & Suites

Bedroom in room 203 at Fairfield Inn & Suites

grab bars, a hand-held showerhead and a fold-down shower bench. There's plenty of room to transfer directly to shower, as there are no obstructions in the transfer space. The bathroom features a full five-foot turning radius and the toilet grab bars are located on the back and right walls (as seated). The bathroom also has a roll-under sink.

Room 321 is an executive queen, and it includes the same basic access features as room 225. It's furnished with two 29-inch high queen-sized beds with an access aisle between them, a chest of drawers and a microwave and

Bathroom in room 203 at Fairfield Inn & Suites

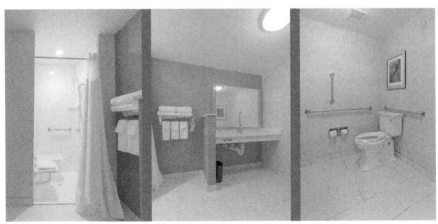

a refrigerator. A separate sitting area includes a 13-inch high sleeper sofa and a desk with a chair.

The bathroom is equipped with a tub/shower combination with grab bars and a hand-held showerhead. A portable shower bench is available upon request. The toilet grab bars are located on the back and left walls (as seated), and the bathroom also has a roll-under sink and a lowered robe hook.

Room 101, which is located on the ground floor, is a standard king. It includes the same basic access features as room 225, and it's the most accessible room at the property. It's furnished with a 29-inch high king-sized bed with wheelchair access on both sides, a desk with a chair, and a chest of drawers. It also includes a refrigerator and a microwave.

The bathroom includes a full five-foot turning radius, and it's equipped with a roll-in shower with grab bars, a hand-held showerhead and a slatted shower bench. The toilet grab bars are located on the back and left walls (as seated), and the bathroom also has a roll-under sink.

There's elevator access to all floors, and barrier-free access to the public areas including the lobby area and the fitness center. There's level access to the lift-equipped indoor pool and spa, and to the adjacent accessible restroom. There's also an accessible restroom located near the lobby.

And if you'd like a bite to eat, Oregano's restaurant is located midway between this

Bedroom in room 321 at Fairfield Inn & Suites

Sitting area in room 321 at Fairfield Inn & Suites

Bedroom in room 101 at Fairfield Inn & Suites

Bathroom in room 101 at Fairfield Inn & Suites

property and the Hampton Inn. There's also a gas station next to the restaurant.

It's a very comfortable property with great access features and nearby visitor services.

Little America Hotel

2515 E. Butler Avenue
Flagstaff, AZ 86004
(928) 779-7900
flagstaff.littleamerica.com

This Flagstaff mainstay has been a visitor favorite for over 45 years; and the good news is, they've consistently added access upgrades, so today it's one of the most accessible properties in the area. There's accessible parking near the main lobby building with ramp access up to the automatic door entrance, and barrier-free access to the spacious lobby. This 247-room property boasts 10 accessible rooms — three with roll-in showers, two with transfer showers, and five with tub/shower combinations.

The guest rooms are spread out in separate lodge buildings throughout the property, with Lodge 1 being the closest to the main lobby. There's level access to this lodge from the main building, and accessible parking near the lodge entrance, which is equipped with an automatic door. Five of the accessible rooms — including room 127 are located in this building.

Room 127 features wide doorways, a lowered peephole, lever handles and good pathway access. It's furnished with two 30-inch high queen-sized beds with wheelchair access between them, two easy chairs, a desk with a chair,

Bedroom in room 127 at Little America Hotel

and a chest of drawers. It also includes a refrigerated drawer, a microwave and a safe.

The bathroom is equipped with a roll-in shower with grab bars, a hand-held showerhead and a fold-down shower seat. The toilet grab bars are located on the back and right walls (as seated), and the bathroom also has a roll-under sink and a lowered robe hook.

Room 214 is also located in Lodge 1, and it includes the same basic access

Bathroom in room 127 at Little America Hotel

features as room 127. It's furnished with two 30-inch high queen-sized beds with wheelchair access between them and on the right side (as you face them), a desk with a chair, two easy chairs and a chest of drawers. A 14-inch high sleeper sofa, two easy chairs and a coffee table are located in the adjacent sitting area; and this room also has a refrigerated drawer, a microwave and a safe.

The bathroom has a 36-inch-square transfer-type shower, with grab bars, a hand-held showerhead and a fold-down shower seat. There's plenty of clear transfer space in this spacious bathroom, which also has a full five-foot turning radius. The toilet grab bars are located on the back and right walls (as seated), and the bathroom also has a roll-under sink.

Room 302 is located in newly renovated Lodge 4; and although it's a bit further from the main lobby, there's accessible parking near the lodge, and a barrier-free path to the automatic door entrance. Room 302 includes the same basic access features as room 127. It's furnished with a 30-inch high queen-sized bed with wheelchair access on both sides, a desk with a chair, an easy chair, a chest of drawers and a 14-inch high sleeper sofa. It also includes a refrigerated drawer, a microwave and a safe.

The bathroom is equipped with a tub/shower combination with grab bars, a hand-held showerhead and a portable shower bench. The toilet grab bars

Bedroom in room 214 at Little America Hotel

Sitting area in room 214 at Little America Hotel

are located on the back and right walls (as seated), and the bathroom also has a roll-under sink.

Room 305, which is located down the hall, has the same basic access features and furnishings as room 302, except that the bathtub also has a ledge seat on the far side of the faucet.

There's elevator access to all floors at this property; and barrier-free access to the public areas including the fitness center, gift shop, and guest

Bathroom in room 214 at Little America Hotel

computer in the lobby. There's also level access to the outdoor lift-equipped pool and spa, which are pleasantly surrounded by pine trees. The Silver Pine restaurant, which is located near the lobby, is open for breakfast, lunch and dinner. It offers level access and plenty of room to maneuver a wheelchair. There are also wheelchair-accessible restrooms located near the lobby.

Little America is a comfortable property, with updated access features and a long history of serving Flagstaff visitors. And even though you're in the middle of the city, you'd never know it from looking at their expansive pine-studded grounds.

Dining

Brandy's Restaurant & Bakery

1500 E. Cedar Avenue #40
Flagstaff, AZ 86004
(928) 779-2187
www.brandysrestaurant.com

There's accessible parking in the nearby lot and barrier-free access to this strip mall cafe that was featured on *Diners, Drive-Ins and Dives*. Table and booth seating are offered inside, with ample room to maneuver a wheelchair around the furniture. There's also an accessible restroom in the back of the restaurant. Open for breakfast and lunch, the menu features a large offering of Benedicts, several breakfast burritos, standard breakfast fare and an interesting mimosa flight. All entrees come with a choice of a homemade buttermilk pancake (the servers' shirts are proudly adorned with "Peace, Love & Pancakes"), or their southwestern take on country potatoes. A good variety of sandwiches, as well as salads and fresh homemade soup are available at lunch; and if you'd like a cookie, muffin or roll to go, the bakery counter is located near the front of the store.

Salsa Brava

2220 E. Route 66
Flagstaff, AZ 86004
(928) 779-5293
www.salsabravaflagstaff.com

Accessible parking is available in front of this Mexican restaurant, which was also featured on *Diners, Drive-Ins and Dives*. There's level access to the front door and plenty of room to maneuver a wheelchair around the tables. Accessible restrooms are located in the back. The menu features a host of Mexican specialties, and the restaurant includes a excellent salsa bar.

The plates are rather large, so if you have a small appetite, then hit up the cantina for happy hour, where you can get two tacos for a reasonable price. The smoked chicken enchiladas and tacos are yummy, and the salsa verde is the real thing. And the fish tacos and red salsa are nothing to sneeze at either. This restaurant is a Flagstaff must-stop for sure.

Black Bart's Steakhouse

2760 E. Butler
Flagstaff, AZ 86004
(928) 779-3142
www.facebook.com/blackbartssteakhouse

Located off Interstate 40, just down the street from Little America, Black Bart's Steakhouse is a tour bus favorite, as it features a decidedly western atmosphere with live musical entertainment by the servers. Like most steakhouses it excels in the meat department, and although there are a few chicken, fish and vegetable choices, they definitely play second fiddle to the beef and pork entrees. The restaurant is located at the back of a RV park, and although there's ample signage on the road, there's also a long dirt road back to the restaurant, which leaves many a visitor wondering if they've made the right turn.

There's plenty of accessible parking near the entrance, with level access to the restaurant. Inside, there's table and chair seating, with ample room to maneuver a wheelchair between the tables. There's also a wheelchair-accessible family restroom near the stage area. The menu features a good selection of sandwiches, burgers, meat entrees and kabobs; and again the beef gets top billing. The serving sizes are also extremely large, so consider a split plate if you aren't hungry enough to eat a horse (which they don't serve).

Nearby

San Francisco Peaks Scenic Road

The stretch of Highway 180 from Flagstaff to Valle features good views of the western slopes of the San Francisco Peaks — including Mt. Humphreys — and makes for a nice scenic drive to or from the South Entrance of Grand Canyon National Park. The route travels through the Coconino National Forest and features a distinctive landscape change — from sagebrush to a pine forest — as the elevation increases. There are numerous pullouts along this 51-mile drive, which takes about an hour to complete. Keep an eye out for elk if you travel the road in the early morning or late afternoon. The road is open all year, but chains may be required in the winter.

Sunset Crater Volcano National Monument

(928) 526-0502

www.nps.gov/sucr

Located 13 miles north of Flagstaff, Sunset Crater Volcano National Monument offers visitors a peek at an ancient eruption along the Lava Flow Trail. Although the entire length of the trail is not accessible, a quarter-mile paved loop is wide and level, and dotted with benches. Halfway along the trail there's an accessible viewing platform which offers a good look at the mountain that exploded over 900 years ago. Along the trail you can spot signs of the eruption, such as limestone fragments that rose with the magma and are now embedded in the surrounding rocks. Accessible picnic tables and restrooms are located back near the parking lot, so this site also makes a good lunch stop.

Wupatki National Monument

25137 N. Wupatki Loop Road

Flagstaff, AZ 86004

(928) 679-2365

www.nps.gov/wupa

Wupatki Pueblo, is also worth a visit while you are at Sunset Crater, as it's just a short 35-mile drive away. As you near the site, the elevation drops 2,000 feet, and the Ponderosa Pine dotted hills give way to red rocks and a painted desert landscape.

The first pueblo you'll spot is Wukoki Pueblo, which is located near the south entrance of the monument. There's a small asphalt parking area without striping, and accessible vault toilets nearby. You can get a good view of the 800-year old ruins from the parking lot, but the access out to the site is blocked by a large step. This Hopi site — which was named for the word for "big house" — was occupied by three families from 1120 to 1210.

Back out on the loop road, the visitor center is the next stop. There's accessible parking in front with level access to the building, and barrier-free access to the gift shop, ranger information desk and accessible restroom inside. An accessible picnic table is located in the front, and there's level access to the accessible Loop Trail in back.

The half-mile trail overlooks the largest pueblo in the monument — Wupatki Pueblo — and offers wheelchair-users and slow walkers an excellent view of the ruins. This 100-room pueblo was occupied by 85 to 100 people in 1182, and it also contains a community room and a

Wupatki Pueblo

ballcourt. And although this sacred site is not physically occupied today, the Hopi people believe their ancestors remain there as spiritual guardians. Interestingly enough, it was also used as a filming location for *Easy Rider*.

The Lomaki site, which is located down the road near the exit, features accessible parking with accessible vault toilets nearby. A half-mile hard-packed dirt trail covered in crushed gravel leads out to the ruins, but the entire length is not accessible. The first part — about .1-mile out to the Box Canyon ruins — is doable, but after that the trail gets steep and loses its access. Still it's worth the short walk to the first site, but be sure and wear sun protection as there's no shade and the desert sun can get intense.

As you near the exit to Wupatki National Monument, the loop road reconnects to Highway 89, about 15 miles north of the entrance to Sunset Crater Volcano National Monument, so it's easy to take in both Sunset Crater and Wupatki Pueblo and then make an easy loop back to Flagstaff.

Walnut Canyon National Monument

(928) 526-3367
www.nps.gov/waca

Located 10 miles east of downtown Flagstaff off Interstate 40, Walnut Canyon was home to the Sinagua people some 800 years ago. Today a few remnants of their occupation remain; however the big attraction at this

Rim Trail at Walnut Canyon National Monument

national monument is the beautiful canyon view. And since it's just a short jog off the highway, it's worth a stop on any east-west journey.

Accessible parking is located near the visitor center, with barrier-free access to the building, and lift access down to the main level. Interpretive exhibits and a short movie acquaint visitors with the history of Walnut Canyon, while rangers are on duty to field questions. There's lift access down to a sun room that offers a beautiful canyon view, and accessible restrooms are located near the entrance.

The .35-mile Rim Trail begins in the front of the visitor center. This paved undulating trail is fairly accessible until the .2-mile mark, where there is a 60-foot section with a marked downhill slope. Although power wheelchairs and scooters won't likely have a problem with the grade, manual wheelchair-users will probably require assistance. There's a nice overlook with benches at the end of the trail, but even if you can't make it that far, there's an equally enticing view at the .1-mile point. And if you'd like to enjoy lunch on the canyon, there's an accessible picnic table on an asphalt pad near the Rim Trail.

Sedona

Known for its red rock formations and vortex sites, Sedona is located 30 miles south of Flagstaff, along Highway 89A. Not only does this mystical locale offer some beautiful windshield views, but there are also a number of accessible trails and overlooks in the land that surrounds the town.

Red Rock Scenic Byway

Although it's less than 10 miles long, this stretch of Highway 179 south of Sedona offers some of the most magnificent views of the red rock formations that line the road. It officially begins at Mile Post 302 and winds past the visitor center and through the Village of Oak Creek. There are several pullouts along the way, where you can get out of your car and take it all in; however the windshield views are nothing to sneeze at either. If you have time stop at Bell Rock and Courthouse Butte to admire the expansive scenery.

Red Rock State Park

4050 Red Rock Loop Road
Sedona, AZ 86336
(928) 282-6907
www.azstateparks.com/red-rock

Located west of town, off Highway 89A, Red Rock State Park is worth a visit

Sedona, Arizona

while you're in the area. That said, go early in the day, as there's not a lot of shade on one of the most accessible trails in the park, and the sun can get pretty severe. It should also be noted that this is a hiking park, and there aren't really any scenic drives or drive-to overlooks there.

There's accessible parking near the visitor center, with ramp access down to the building. Inside there's plenty of room to maneuver a wheelchair around the gift shop, ranger information desk and interpretive exhibits. Accessible restrooms are located near the front door, and there's also level access to the theater and classroom next door. And don't miss the hummingbird garden on the back patio of the classroom.

The accessible Mesquite Trail is located near the parking lot, and it features a paved level pathway around interpretive plaques about the native plants. There's a shaded picnic area with accessible tables near the trail; and there's also a shade structure located in the middle of this quarter-mile trail.

The longer Bunkhouse Trail begins behind the visitor center; and although you can get to it from the parking lot, that pathway has a steep grade, so it's best to access the trail from the hummingbird garden behind the classroom. The paved trail is fairly level, although there is a bit of a grade in the beginning. Power wheelchair-users won't have a problem, but some manual wheelchair-users may require assistance. There are also some cracks along the paved trail, but other than that it's fairly smooth rolling. At about the .2-mile mark there's an accessible hard-packed dirt trail down to the Kingfisher Bridge, which provides a pleasant — and shaded — view of Oak Creek. From there a hard-packed dirt path follows the creek for another .2 mile before the trail loses its access. All in all it's about a mile round-trip hike; but you can do as little or as much of the route as you want.

Slide Rock State Park

6871 N. Highway 89A
Sedona, AZ 86336
(928) 282-3034
www.azstateparks.com/slide-rock

A favorite local haunt, this park provides access to Oak Creek, and it takes its name from the rocks that many folks use as slides to get into the water. Unfortunately the path down to the creek is not accessible, but there is a short trail that offers a scenic overlook of the canyon. That said, the admission is pretty steep (currently $20 per car) for just that trail;

however if you have an Arizona State Park Pass, this park makes a nice lunch stop.

There's accessible parking near the shaded picnic area — which has several accessible tables — and barrier-free access over to the Pendley Homestead Trail. This paved level trail leads past a small store, and by a display of vintage farming equipment, over to the old homestead which has a tractor display in the adjacent barn. It then connects with the Cliff Top Trail which has a 75-foot paved path out to an accessible overlook that offers an expansive view of Oak Creek Canyon. All in all it's about a quarter-mile round trip, and it makes for a nice stroll before of after lunch. The red rock vistas are equally impressive from the picnic area, so you don't even have to hike to get a good view in this park.

Out of Africa

3505 W. SR 260
Camp Verde, AZ 86322
(928) 567-2840
www.outofafricapark.com

Located 30 miles south of Sedona, this this 100-acre refuge is home to hundreds of mammals, birds and reptiles from around the world. But Out of Africa is more than just a zoo or preserve, as the founder's mission is to raise awareness of these exotic creatures and help visitors understand their behaviors through personal contact.

There are several things to do in the park, but by far the most popular attraction is the African Bush Safari. This 40-minute tour is conducted in an open-air bus, which travels through the 25-acre Masai Mara enclosure. The bus features ramp access and has wheelchair spaces with tie-downs. The guides point out the wildlife along the way — including zebras, antelope and giraffes — and slow down or stop for photos.

It's also possible to walk along the main park road; however even though it's paved it has a few steep patches. Alternatively, a wheelchair-accessible tram runs along the road and stops at many of the popular enclosures, most of which offer barrier-free access. Make sure and have a look at the reptile house, and the leopards, lions, tigers and servals; and don't miss the prairie dog village and the macaw house.

Additionally there are many animal demonstrations and shows throughout the day, but be sure and catch the signature Tiger Splash show. This captivating presentation features Bengal and Siberian Tigers that interact

Accessible tram at Out of Africa

with their caretakers and present predator-and-play behaviors in the water. There's level access to Tiger Splash Arena from the tram stop, and plenty of accessible seating up close to the action in the first row. This popular show is only presented once each day, so be sure and check the schedule when you first get to the park.

Montezuma Castle National Monument

Highway 17
Camp Verde, AZ 86322
(928) 567-3322 X221
www.nps.gov/moca

Located off Highway 17 near Camp Verde, Montezuma Castle National Monument is worth a quick stop while you're in the area. There's accessible parking in front, with level access over to the visitor center. Inside there's barrier-free access to the interpretive exhibits, ranger information desk and gift shop. Accessible restrooms are located near the entrance.

Out back there's a half-mile paved trail that offers visitors a good view of the cliff dwellings that are precariously perched on the hillside above the site. The trail has a few dips, but aside from one steep path out to a viewing platform, it's still quite doable for wheelchair-users and slow walkers. Constructed by the Sinagua people over 600 years ago, this five-story structure once contained approximately 45 rooms. Today the ruins have deteriorated a bit

Cliff dwellings at Montezuma Castle National Monument

since early American settlers first discovered it, however it's still an impressive site. Interpretive plaques are located along the trail; and an intricately crafted diorama located near the visitor center offers visitors a good interpretation of these ancient ruins. As an added bonus, the trail is partially shaded by the bordering forest, so it's a pleasant stop on a warm day. And although sunrise or sunset would be impressive at this site, Montezuma Castle is only open from 8:00 a.m. to 5:00 p.m., so plan accordingly.

Verde Canyon Railroad

300 N. Broadway
Clarkdale, AZ 86324
(800) 528-7245
www.verdecanyonrr.com

If you'd like a great view of the red rock country in the Sedona area, but want to sit back and leave the driving to someone else, then plan for a day excursion on the very scenic Verde Canyon Railroad. Departing from Clarkdale station, this four-hour excursion offers visitors an up-close-and-personal look at what's often been billed as "Arizona's other Grand Canyon".

Accessible parking is located near the station, with ramp access up to the departure area, which includes the ticket office, a gift shop, the Copper Spike Cafe, and a covered outdoor patio — all of which offer barrier-free access.

There's also ramp access up to the John Bell Museum and plenty of room to maneuver a wheelchair around the adjacent storyboards, which together offer a good primer on local railroad history. Accessible restrooms are located near the ticket office, and the large restroom building near the museum also has an accessible family restroom. And if you'd like to pick up a quick snack, there's also level access to the Whistlestop convenience store.

When boarding time comes, the staff is happy to give slow walkers a golf cart ride to their car, as sometimes the train can be quite long. Three of the rail cars — one coach and two first class — have an on-board lift. This allows wheelchair-users access to the open-air car as well as the adjacent air conditioned passenger car. The lift has a capacity of 500 pounds, and there's also a wheelchair available for loan for slow walkers.

Passengers are free to move to the open-air cars during the journey, and all of the accessible cars have good pathway access to and from them. Wheelchair-users can transfer to a seat in the passenger car, or opt to stay in their own wheelchair for the journey — the choice is theirs, and the crew is very accommodating. The accessible cars also each have an accessible restroom.

The first class cars offer spacious living-room style seating, and they carry fewer passengers than the coach cars, which have traditional Pullman-style seats. A light lunch is served in first class, and a full bar is also available. Snacks are available for purchase in coach, and everyone gets a great view of

Lift boarding on Verde Canyon Railroad

the changing landscape as the train chugs past Sinagua ruins, along the Verde River, through a 680-foot tunnel and over an iron bridge up to Perkinsville. There's a short stop in Perkinsville — where passengers remain on the train — while the engine is repositioned for the downhill journey. And the great part about the journey is that there's a completely different view on the way back.

It's a great way to spend the afternoon, and the folks at Verde Canyon Railway will do everything in their power to make your journey more enjoyable. That said, remember to let them know what kind of assistance you need when you make your reservation, as it will make things go more smoothly when it comes time to board the train.

Jerome State Park

100 Douglas Road
Jerome, AZ 86331
(928) 634-5381
www.azstateparks.com/jerome

For a good interpretation of the wild and wooly copper mining town of Jerome, be sure and stop by Jerome State Park. Housed in stately Douglas Mansion on the outskirts of this reborn ghost town, this museum includes artifacts from the boom days, and includes extensive mining exhibits. Accessible parking is available near the entrance, with ramp access up to the museum. Inside there's ample room to maneuver a wheelchair around the first-floor exhibits, but only stairway access to the second-floor mining exhibit in this historic building. There's accessible seating in the theater, where a 28-minute film that details the history of Jerome is shown. The downstairs rooms include objects from Jerome's past, and many are decorated with period furnishings. There's also level access to the outdoor exhibits, which include everything from a stamp mill and an arrastra, to depression era mining equipment, old mining cars and even a carriage house with a vintage buggy and a Model A Ford. There's also a shaded picnic area near the entrance which has accessible tables, so it's a good place to stop for an al fresco lunch break.

Dead Horse Ranch State Park

675 Dead Horse Ranch Road
Cottonwood, AZ 86326
(928) 634-5283
www.azstateparks.com/dead-horse

Located just four miles from Clarkdale, Dead Horse Ranch State Park makes a nice stop on the way to or from Verde Canyon Railroad. And if you'd like to spend the night there, they also have some affordable and accessible camping cabins.

Although the name sounds rather unappealing, there's an interesting story behind it all. Back in the 1940s the Ireys family came west in search of a better life. After several days of hunting for the perfect ranch, Mr. Ireys asked his kids which place they liked best. The children excitedly replied, "The one with the dead horse in front of it, dad." And with that response, the family found a new home, and subsequently renamed it to mark the momentous occasion. Thirty years later, when Arizona State Parks acquired the parcel, retention of the colorful name was a condition of the sale.

Trails

The park is a prime birding spot in the spring and fall, and the headquarters for the Verde Valley Birding & Nature Festival in late April. The best place to get a glance of the avian residents is on the Canopy Trail, which begins in the day use area. Accessible parking is located near the trailhead, and although it's a short walk from the cabins, there are stairs and other obstacles along the way, so it's best to drive.

The quarter-mile wheelchair-accessible trail has a hard-packed dirt surface and is covered in crushed granite. The wide level trail winds under a cottonwood canopy, so there's also plenty of shade along the way. There are even a few cement sections, and the whole trail is designated as a
Canopy Trail at Dead Horse Ranch State Park

"smoke-free and herbicide-free zone" to accommodate people with multiple chemical sensitivity. About halfway along the loop there's a picnic table and a large collection of chairs under an enormous cottonwood tree. There are also several hummingbird feeders in the area, so it's the ideal place to just sit back and wait for the birds to appear. And if you'd like to pack along a picnic lunch, there are some sheltered picnic tables on a cement pad near the accessible restrooms in the parking lot.

Another must-see in the park are the three lagoons located near the end of the main park road. Filled with water from the Verde River, these lagoons are stocked with catfish and trout, and feature accessible trails around them. The trail around the west lagoon is a third-mile long, while the trail around the middle lagoon measures nearly a half-mile. And if you'd prefer a three-quarter mile scenic stroll, then the trail around the east lagoon is just what the doctor ordered.

There's plenty of accessible parking around all of the lagoons, with barrier-free access to the lagoon trails, which also act as levees. The hard-packed dirt trails are wide and level, and they are shaded by trees that dot the shore. There are also several accessible fishing piers on each lagoon that offer roll-on access and lowered rails. Additionally if you'd like a longer walk, the trails connect, so you can plan a round-trip hike around all three lagoons.

Fishing pier at Dead Horse Ranch State Park

Cabins

There are also several accessible camping cabins in the park. Cabin 1 (also known as Antelope) has a paved parking area in front, with level access up to the front porch. There's is a wide doorway and adequate wheelchair clearance inside the cabin. It's furnished with a set of bunk beds and a double bed, a chest of drawers, a table and four chairs. The bunk bed is 17 inches high, while the double bed is 23 inches high; and they both offer wheelchair access on one side. Additionally, the chairs can be easily stowed on hooks when not in use, which frees up more floor space. The cabin also has electricity, overhead lights and an air conditioner. Outside there's a picnic table on a level grassy area next to the cabin. There is also a fire grill near the table, and a bench on the porch.

There are three other accessible cabins, including cabin 2 (Bobcat), cabin 5 (Eagle) and cabin 8 (Hawk). They all have the same configuration as cabin 1, but cabin 5 offers the most privacy.

The bathhouse is located a short walk away along the paved road. The large family restroom includes a roll-in shower with a fold-down shower bench and grab bars. The shower is large, and the bench is four-feet from the shower faucet, so this setup is best for someone who has their own shower chair or has an assistant. There's no hand-held showerhead, and as a water conservation measure, a one-to-two minute water spurt is released when the

Antelope cabin at Dead Horse Ranch State Park

Inside the Antelope cabin at Dead Horse Ranch State Park

Family restroom in the bathhouse at Dead Horse Ranch State Park

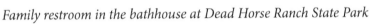

shower knob is pressed. It can be pressed with a fist, and although it seems inconvenient, at least it's free. There's also a toilet with grab bars on the back and right walls (as seated), and a roll-under sink in the bathroom.

The cabins are pretty basic, but they're a good choice if you want a real nature experience. Steer clear of the area in the summer though, as the mercury rises drastically and the daytime temperatures are oppressive at best.

Winslow

Elevation 4,850 feet

L ocated about 90 miles east of Williams along Interstate 40, Winslow is about a 2.5-hour drive from the South Rim. Even though it's a bit too far for a day trip to the national park, it's still worth a stopover on the way to or from the Grand Canyon. It's a must-see for anyone interested in railroad history, and a fun Route 66 stop. It's also a good home base for a visit to nearby Petrified Forest National Park.

Attractions

Lorenzo Hubbell Trading Post & Visitor Center

523 W. 2nd Street
Winslow, AZ 86047
(928) 289-2434

Located on the west side of town, this visitor center is housed in what was once the premier trading post in the American Southwest. There's accessible parking near this historic building; and although steps grace the entrance, there is also a wheelchair lift on the side. Inside there's plenty of room to maneuver a wheelchair around the historic displays

Harvey House – La Posada

and the racks of information on Arizona attractions. The exhibits include everything from a Kachina doll collection and an old freight scale to historic photos and even a guitar signed by the Eagles. The visitor center is staffed by helpful volunteers who will point you in the right direction, and there are accessible restrooms near the door. And if you just want a cold drink of water, they have that too.

Harvey House — La Posada

303 E. 2nd Street
Winslow, AZ 86047
(928) 289-4366
www.laposada.org

Built in 1929, La Posada quickly became known as one of the finest lodging establishments in the southwest. This famed Harvey House, which was designed by Grand Canyon architect Mary Colter, was said to be one of her favorites. Since Winslow was the Arizona headquarters for the Santa Fe Railroad, no expense was spared in the construction of the property; and when it was all said and done the budget topped $2 million (which translates to about $40 million today).

The restaurant and hotel are still operational today (see below); but this local landmark is worth a stop even if you don't spend the night. The property is filled with nooks and crannies that contain historic photographs and artifacts; and although the historic building lacks an elevator, most of the exhibits are located on the first floor. Highlights include vintage Winslow photos, Harvey House tableware, Indian pottery and contemporary artwork.

Standing on the Corner Park

2nd Street & Kinsley
Winslow, AZ 86047
www.standinonthecorner.com

Located on the corner of 2nd Street (Route 66) and Kinsley, this roadside attraction brings to life the lyrics in *Take it Easy*, the 1970 Eagles hit. It features a mural by John Pugh, which depicts the famous lyrics — "a girl, my lord, in a flat bed Ford slowin' down to take a look at me." There is also a bronze sculpture by Ron Adamson of a musician with a guitar (known locally as "Easy") "standing on a corner in Winslow, Arizona" in front of the mural. Another sculpture of Glenn Frey was added nearby in 2016. There's level access along the walkway in front of the mural, and barrier-free access to the surrounding stores which hawk kitschy Route 66 souvenirs. And if

Standing on the Corner Park

you're lucky, you'll also hear strains of the hit tune coming from one of the stores. There's also level access to the new park, complete with a stage, on the other side of Kinsley Avenue. Accessible parking is located in the public lot at 2nd and Williamson, which is just a level block away.

Old Trails Museum

212 N. Kinsley Avenue
Winslow, AZ 86047
(928) 289-5861
www.oldtrailsmuseum.org

Located on Kinsley Avenue, down the street from the musical corner, the Old Trails Museum offers an interesting look at the city's history. Housed in an old bank building — complete with a vault — the museum offers level access and room enough for a wheelchair to maneuver around the display cases. Highlights include exhibits on the Santa Fe Railroad, Fred Harvey and the La Posada, prominent locals, vintage toys and of course Route 66. Local volunteers help put a personal spin on the artifacts, and there's no shortage of historic photos of Winslow. Best of all there's no admission charge to this home town museum.

Burma Shave signs on the 1st Street Walkway

Trails

1st Street Walkway

This half-mile paved pathway leads from the visitor center along 1st street, and ends at a gazebo across from Kinsley Avenue. There's also a ramped train exhibit about halfway along the walkway at Winslow Avenue. Although these Santa Fe train cars are not open, visitors can roll up on the platform for a better look at them. From the gazebo at Kinsley Avenue, visitors can walk the level block down to 2nd Street (Route 66) to Standing on the Corner Park. There's curb-cut access to the sidewalks, and it's a nice level roll down to the infamous corner. This new trail is very nicely done access-wise, and it includes Burma Shave-like signs and a pleasant greenbelt along the way.

Lodging

La Posada

303 E. 2nd Street
Winslow, AZ 86047
(928) 289-4366
www.laposada.org

Access is good throughout this historic property, with accessible parking in front, and a level sidewalk to the front entrance. Even though the sidewalk is a bit on the long side, there are also benches to sit down and rest along the way. Inside, there's level access to the front lobby and gift shop, and a barrier-free pathway to room 116, which is located on the first floor.

The room features wide doorways and tile floors, and good pathway access on both sides of the 26-inch high king-sized bed. It's decorated in a traditional southwestern style and there are even some old Harvey House photos on the wall. A large roll-under sink and vanity occupies one wall of the guest room, while a desk and chair are located near the foot of the bed.

The spacious bathroom is equipped with a large roll-in shower with a hand-held showerhead and grab bars. The tiled shower is very nicely done, and it's a whopping three feet deep and nearly five feet wide. Top it off with toilet grab bars on the back and right walls (as seated), and a portable shower chair, and you have a very accessible room.

There's barrier-free access to most of the first floor public areas as well, including the gift shop, restaurant and lobby areas. The lobby level galleries include historic photos, displays of Indian pottery, some contemporary art, and vintage furniture and decorations. Even if you don't stay at the property save some time to pop in and browse through the galleries. There's level access to this first-floor area (and the restaurant) through the gift shop.

Bedroom in room 116 at La Posada

Bathroom in room 116 at La Posada

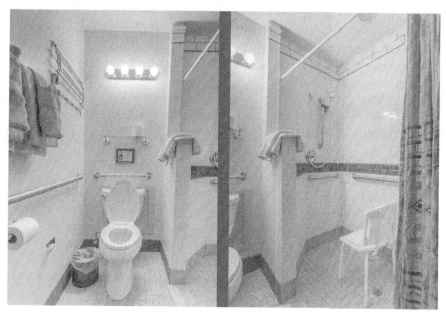

Dining

Turquoise Room

303 E. 2nd Street
Winslow, AZ 86047
(928) 289-2888
www.theturquoiseroom.net

Located just off the lobby of the Las Posada this former Harvey House restaurant now serves up a nice selection of southwestern favorites with the occasional tribute to Fred Harvey thrown in for good measure. The waitresses are dressed in traditional Harvey House uniforms, and the Turquoise Room welcomes guests for breakfast, lunch and dinner. There's level access to the restaurant and adjacent bar, with plenty of room to maneuver a wheelchair. As an added bonus the restaurant faces the railroad tracks, so you get the real Harvey House experience, especially when a train passes.

Las Marias

122 E. 2nd Street
Winslow, AZ 86047
(928) 289-6496

Located on the main drag, across from the public parking area, this taco shop offers enchiladas, tacos, burritos and other Mexican favorites. There's a ramp of sorts that leads to the patio, but most wheelers will need assistance with the slope. Inside there's level access to the counter and room for a wheelchair to maneuver around the tables. A good place for a quick and cheap meal, Las Marias is open for breakfast, lunch and dinner.

Brown Mug Café

308 E. 2nd Street
Winslow, AZ 86047
(928) 289-9973

This local favorite is located across the street from La Posada. There's no accessible parking in the small lot, but there's room to parallel park an adapted van on the street. Alternatively, accessible parking spaces are available at La Posada. Open for breakfast, lunch and dinner, this long-time Winslow favorite features doable access through the front door and a lowered counter which will work for wheelchair-users. There's also space at the end of one booth that that may work for some folks. The bathroom is doable for manual wheelchair-users, but folks with power wheelchairs or scooters may have trouble closing the door. The Brown Mug serves up some tasty Mexican fare, and also has burgers and sandwiches on the menu. It can get crowded at high noon, so plan for an earlier or later lunch for the best seat selection.

Sipp Shoppe

101 W. 2nd Street
Winslow, AZ 86047
(928) 289-2534
www.facebook.com/SippShoppe

Located across from Standing on the Corner Park, this soda fountain offers sandwiches, burgers, coffee drinks, sodas and ice cream treats. There's barrier-free access through the front door, and room to maneuver a wheelchair around the tables. Accessible restrooms are located at the end of a ramp in the back of the building. The Sipp Shoppe is a good place to wet your whistle on a hot day, and it also has some vintage Winslow photos on display.

Brown Mug Cafe

Nearby

Homolovi State Park

Arizona 87
Winslow, AZ 86047
(928) 289-4106
www.azstateparks.com/homolovi

Located on Highway 87, a few miles north of Interstate 40, these ancient ruins make a good stand-alone trip, as well as an interesting side trip on the way to the Hopi Second Mesa. There's accessible parking in the visitor center parking lot, with barrier-free access to the building. Inside, there's ample room to maneuver a wheelchair around the interpretive exhibits, ranger information desk and small gift shop. Accessible restrooms are located near the information desk, and there are a few accessible picnic tables on the back patio. There's also level access out to a viewpoint where you can get a gander at an excavated pueblo, but because of a rocky pathway you can't roll out to it.

The main ruins are located a few miles away at Homolovi II. There's accessible parking with curb-cut access out to a quarter-mile paved path that leads out to these Anasazi ruins, which are believed to have been inhabited by Hopi ancestors some 700 years ago. The ruins includes the remains of a central plaza, kiva and five-room pueblo, with pottery shards

Ruins at Homolovi State Park

strewn over the whole area. And the views of the desert, mesas and San Francisco peaks are spectacular from just about any spot along the trail. There are benches to sit and enjoy the views, and an accessible picnic table in a shaded ramada near the beginning of the trail. It's definitely the picnic area with a view, so don't forget to pack along a lunch. And if that picnic area is occupied, there are also two shaded accessible tables located between the visitor center and Homolovi II that offer equally scenic lunchtime views.

Ash Fork Route 66 Museum

901 West Old Route 66
Ash Fork, Arizona 86320
Phone: (928) 637-0204
www.facebook.com/AshForkHistoricalSociety

Operated by the Ash Fork Historical Society, the Ash Fork Route 66 Museum is worth a stop on any Mother Road pilgrimage. It's located right off Interstate 40, about 20 miles west of Williams in sleepy little Ash Fork. There's accessible parking in front of the museum, which is housed in a former Route 66 maintenance building, and level access to the entrance. Inside there's plenty of room to maneuver a wheelchair or scooter around the exhibits. Highlights include old cars, tools and signs, as well as an impressive collection of railroad memorabilia. There's also a nice model of the old Escalante Hotel, which operated from 1907 to 1968, and was considered to be the best Harvey House west of Chicago. Top it off with a large Kachina collection, some vintage glass and even an old jail cell, and you have a comprehensive showcase of the Route 66 boom days. There's also a visitor center in the front lobby, and a nice accessible restroom near the museum entrance. Best of all, there's no admission charge, but plan ahead as this fun museum is only open on weekdays.

Hopi-Navajo Reservation Scenic Drive

This loop drive makes an excellent day trip from Winslow, and it offers some great windshield views and gives visitors the opportunity to pick up handcrafted Hopi wares along the way. From Interstate 40, head north on Highway 87 past Homolovi State Park and across the Painted Desert. It's about an hour-drive to the Second Mesa on the Hopi reservation, and you can clearly see the three Hopi mesas in the distance as you travel up this two-lane scenic highway.

When you hit Highway 264, turn left and continue along the scenic route. At this point the desert gives way to canyon views, and you'll see homes and other buildings along the roadside. If you'd like to shop for native baskets or Katsina dolls, stop at the Tsakurshovi Gallery, which is located near Mile Post 381 on the right side of the road. There's no striped parking in the dirt lot, but there's usually plenty of room to park an adapted van. The gallery is small, but there is level access, and the owners are happy to show you wares that may be out of reach. They also enjoy talking about their culture and the area.

Be sure and stop at the Hopi Cultural Center, which is up the road a few miles. There's accessible parking in the paved lot near the buildings, with barrier-free access to the Hopi Museum, restaurant and galleries. The restroom near the restaurant has a small stall with grab bars; however the newer one near the museum offers excellent access. Even if you don't want to visit the museum or eat, make sure and use this site as a rest stop as there really aren't any other accessible public toilet facilities on the reservation.

The museum itself is definitely worth a visit though, as it houses a eclectic collection of historic and contemporary artifacts, including Katsina dolls, pottery, baskets and jewelry. The highlight of the exhibition however is the collection of old photographs that show the Hopi at work and play, which gives visitors some insight into the culture. Save some time to browse through the galleries near the museum, which all offer level access and barrier-free pathways.

And if you'd like to shop for Hopi inlay jewelry, make sure and stop at the Monongya Gallery, located about seven miles up the road on the left, in the

Hopi Cultural Center on the Hopi-Navajo Reservation Drive

village of Orayvi. There's plenty of parking in the level lot, and although there is a cement ramp up to the entrance, it's steep and manual wheelchair-users will definitely need some assistance. Once inside there's plenty of room to maneuver a wheelchair in the spacious gallery which is filled with jewelry cases. Other offerings include, baskets, weavings and rugs.

To make the loop, you'll have to backtrack a bit to Indian Highway 2 — just follow the sign to Leupp. This road crosses through the Navajo reservation and offers some nice windshield views of the surrounding buttes, with the San Francisco peaks in the distance. When you reach the end of the road, make a right on Navajo Highway 15, then take Highway 99 to reconnect to interstate 40, and head east to Winslow. The drive takes about three hours straight through, but with photo stops, shopping and lunch it's really a day-long excursion. Even if you don't stop at any galleries, the windshield views make this drive a must-do.

Petrified Forest National Park

1 Park Road
Petrified Forest, AZ 86028
(928) 524-6228
www.nps.gov/pefo

Located about an hour east of Winslow, Petrified Forest National Park boasts the world's largest concentration of petrified wood, and offers visitors
View at Tawa Point in Petrified Forest National Park

some dazzling desert views. It makes a good break from any Interstate 40 road trip, and it's easy to do a one-way drive through the park and then reconnect with the highway.

If you're traveling east, take the Highway 180 exit (exit 285) and use the south entrance of the park; and if you're traveling west, take exit 311 and use the north entrance. Either way, after you've explored the 28-mile route, you can easily continue along your way. The whole drive takes an hour without any stops, and although there are some wonderful windshield views along the way, there are also some very scenic turnouts and sights that are definitely worth a stop. It should also be noted that the gates to this national park open at 8:00 a.m. and close at 5:00 p.m., so plan accordingly to avoid disappointment.

The Painted Desert Visitor Center, which is located near the north entrance, makes a good first stop in the park. Accessible parking is located near the entrance, with level access to the building, which houses a small gift shop and an ranger information desk. Accessible restrooms are located near the entrance, and there's also level access to the Painted Desert Diner around the corner.

Although there's no shortage of scenic views in the park, make sure and stop at Tawa Point, just past the north entrance, for that first expansive view of the Painted Desert. Accessible parking is located near curb-cut access up to a short .1-mile paved trail out to the viewpoint. The last 20 feet of this path is a

The Painted Desert Inn in Petrified Forest National Park

bit steep for manual wheelchair-users; however you can get a good view of the colorful desert from any place along the trail, or even from the parking lot.

The Painted Desert Inn, which is located just a half-mile up the road, is also worth a stop. This former Harvey House was designed by Mary Colter, and it operated until 1963. There's accessible parking in front and level access to the building, which contains exhibits about the property and features the old dining counter and lunch room, complete with vintage place settings. There's also a great view of the desert from this second-story vantage point. An accessible path winds around to the other side of this split-level structure, where there's barrier-free access to the ground floor ice cream fountain. Accessible restrooms are located next door, and there are several accessible picnic tables on the adjacent patio. There's also a 300-foot paved level pathway out to Kachina Point, but you can get an equally impressive view from the inn and the parking lot as well.

Another worthwhile stop is Puerco Pueblo, which is a few miles up the road, just past the railroad tracks. Accessible parking with curb-cut access up to the sidewalk is located near the accessible vault toilets. From there it's about a 200-foot walk out to a .3-mile paved trail that circles the ruins of these ancestral Puebloan homes that were occupied from 1250 to 1380.

And don't miss Newspaper Rock, which is short drive down the road. That site features a 200-foot paved level trail out to some Puebloan petroglyphs,

Newspaper Rock in Petrified Forest National Park

which were created 2,000 years ago. There's an accessible spotting scope at the overlook, which offers a good view of the 650-plus petroglyphs.

For a great view of a colorful mesa, check out the Blue Mesa overlooks that are located about three miles off the main road, just south of Newspaper Rock. There are a number of pullouts along the drive where you can stop and admire the colorful badlands views, but the windshield views from the road are equally enchanting.

Back on the main park road, there's a substantial collection of petrified wood at the Crystal Forest stop, located a little further south. Although a paved .8-mile trail leads past the petrified logs, because of a maximum 20% grade, it's not a good choice for wheelchair-users and slow walkers. That said there is a 400-foot paved level path that leads out to the trailhead, that offers a good overview of the remains of this ancient forest. Go as far along the trail as possible, but keep in mind that the steepest sections are near the end, so you may have to double back.

Finally, don't miss the Rainbow Forest stop, which is located just north of the south entrance. There's accessible parking near the Rainbow Forest Visitor Center, with ramp access up to the front door. Inside there's barrier-free access to the interpretive exhibits, ranger information desk and accessible restrooms. There's also plenty of room for wheelchairs and scooters in the theater, where a movie about the park is shown throughout

Crystal Forest trail in Petrified Forest National Park

the day. A manual wheelchair is also available for loan on a first-come basis. The Giant Logs Trail is located out back, and although this paved trail starts out level, the access ends 600 feet later at the Mather plaque, where steps block the rest of the route. Still, the view is good from the back of the visitor center too.

And if you'd like a bite to eat, there's level access to a curio shop which offers some snacks at the other end of the parking lot. There's also a covered picnic area located nearby, which has level access to accessible tables.

All in all, this scenic national park is well worth a short detour to or from the Grand Canyon.

Route 66 and Interstate 40 Resources

Kingman Visitor Information
(866) 427-7866
www.gokingman.com

Flagstaff Convention & Visitors Bureau
(928) 213-2951
www.flagstaffarizona.org

Williams Visitor Center
(928) 635-4061
www.experiencewilliams.com

Winslow Chamber of Commerce
(928) 289-2434
www.winslowarizona.org

Tourism Arizona
www.visitarizona.com

Access Resources

Emerging Horizons

www.EmergingHorizons.com

Your one-stop accessible travel resource.

- Destinations
- Lodging Options
- Tour Companies
- Travel News
- Trails & Recreation
- Travel Tips

Barrier-Free National Parks

www.BarrierFreeNationalParks.com

Access information on some of America's top national parks.

- Insider Tips
- Resources
- Suggested Itineraries
- Access Photos

Barrier-Free Travel Yosemite, Sequoia and Kings Canyon National Parks

FOR WHEELERS AND SLOW WALKERS

By Candy B. Harrington

This indispensable guidebook includes detailed access information that will help wheelchair-users and slow walkers find an accessible room and build a barrier-free itinerary in Central California's top three national parks. Along with updated information about accessible trails, boardwalks, viewpoints, museums and picnic areas, this helpful resource also includes detailed access evaluations and photographs of 33 properties in and near the parks. And if you'd like to sleep under the stars, barrier-free campsites are also noted. Add in helpful details about the location of local airports, and the availability of accessible shuttles, public transportation and van rentals, and you've got all the information you need to get to and around the parks. Top it off with information on accessible bus tours, ranger programs, wheelchair and handcycle rentals and you have a must-have resource for wheelchair-users, stroller parents or anybody who just needs to take things a little slower.

www.barrierfreeyosemite.com

Barrier-Free Travel Glacier, Yellowstone and Grand Teton National Parks

FOR WHEELERS AND SLOW WALKERS

By Candy B. Harrington

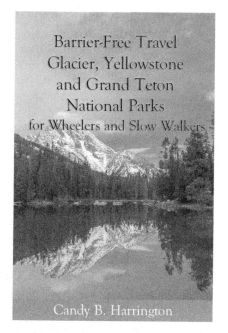

Penned by accessible travel expert Candy B. Harrington, this access guide includes detailed information about accessible trails, picnic areas, lodging options and attractions in Glacier, Yellowstone and Grand Teton National Parks. This handy resource features access details and photos of over 40 lodging options, including all in-park lodgings, as well as gateway city offerings. Details on accessible bus and boat tours, and shuttle service to, from and in the parks are also included. Top it off with information on recent access upgrades, barrier-free camping, and Amtrak, airport and accessible van rental details, and you have a one-stop national park resource. This guide will help you find an accessible room that works for you, and plan a accessible itinerary based on your abilities to these three favorite national parks.

www.barrierfreeyellowstone.com

Barrier-Free Travel
Utah National Parks

FOR WHEELERS AND SLOW WALKERS

By Candy B. Harrington

This handy guide includes detailed information about accessible trails, sites, lodging options, tours, transportation and attractions in Zion, Bryce Canyon, Capitol Reef, Arches and Canyonlands National Parks. Along with detailed information about trails and viewpoints that will work for wheelchair-users and slow walkers, it also includes detailed descriptions of all the in-park lodging options, along with photographs of the accessible rooms. Access details and photos of 23 additional accessible lodging options near the parks are also included, as well as information on accessible campsites in the parks. Top it off with information about ranger-led tours, loaner wheelchairs and the free America the Beautiful Access Pass and you have a very comprehensive resource.

www.barrierfreeutah.com

Barrier-Free Travel
Utah's National Parks
for Wheelers and Slow Walkers

Candy B. Harrington